AFRICAN NATIVE MUSIC.
AN ANNOTATED BIBLIOGRAPHY.

AFRICAN NATIVE MUSIC

AN ANNOTATED BIBLIOGRAPHY

COMPILED BY

DOUGLAS H. VARLEY, B.A.

1970
DAWSONS OF PALL MALL
Folkestone and London

This reprint is authorized by
The Royal Commonwealth Society

First published in 1936
Reprinted 1970

Dawsons of Pall Mall
Cannon House
Folkestone, Kent, England

SBN: 7129 0422 0

*Printed in Great Britain
by Photolithography
Unwin Brothers Limited
Woking and London*

NOTE.

This bibliography deals with African Native Music, but its scope is confined to the Negro and Bantu cultures, roughly south of the Sahara. The entries are arranged geographically; some tribes have for this purpose been arbitrarily split up, although no more arbitrarily than in political reality. Searchers after the music of particular tribes are advised not to neglect the general sections, where comprehensive entries relating to many parts of the continent have been placed (e.g., see Schneider, on page 23). In default of any standard guide to tribal nomenclature, except in the Belgian Congo, the best known names have been preferred in the annotations. It is hoped that the confusion of variants in the entries themselves (including five for the Fang of Middle Congo) will make clearer the urgent need for some authoritative guidance on this subject. A short list of the more useful current bibliographies has been added to assist those who wish to acquaint themselves with the most recent published work on comparative musicology.

The place of publication of all entries is London, except where otherwise stated.

I wish here to acknowledge my indebtedness to Canon Anson Phelps Stokes and Dr. Thomas Jesse Jones, of the Phelps-Stokes Trust, and to Miss G. A. Gollock, the Council and the Library Committee of the Royal Empire Society for their interest and support in this project, and particularly for making possible a visit to the Negro Colleges and chief bibliographical centres in the United States. My thanks are also due to the late Professor Erich von Hornbostel, who examined and usefully criticised the work in manuscript; to Dr. George Herzog of Yale University, Professor Dr. Bernhard Struck of Dresden and Rev. Edwin W. Smith for valuable suggestions and advice; to Mr. W. D. Hambly of the Field Museum, Chicago, Mr. Walter Cline of Harvard, Dr. Monroe Work of Tuskegee, Mr. A. A. Schomburg, Mr. Phillips Barry, Dr. Guy Johnson, Dr. Andrew Hensey of Hartford, and many other American friends, for their hospitality and good counsel; to the Librarians of the Royal Anthropological Institute and the Royal Geographical Society for permission to use their resources; and to Dr. H. Labouret and Miss Margaret Wrong for assistance with the sections on Drum-language and Church Music respectively.

Finally I wish to thank Miss Vera Ward and Miss M. Maynard for help in the preparation of the manuscript, and last but not least Mr. Evans Lewin, for encouragement and advice in every stage of the work.

D. H. V.

October, 1936.

Additional Note

Since this bibliography was compiled and published, much work has been done in the field of African Musicology. A record of this work will be found in the following bibliographies:

MERRIAM, Alan P. An annotated bibliography of African- and African-derived music since 1936. (*Africa*, 21(4), 319–29) October 1951

THIEME, Darius L. *African Music:* a briefly annotated bibliography. Washington, Library of Congress, 1964,

GASKIN, L. J. P. *Select bibliography of music in Africa.* (African bibliographical Series B) London, for ´ International African Institute, 1965

For particulars of recordings of African music, see the journals *Ethnomusicology* and *African Music*.

D. H. V.

UNIVERSITY OF LIVERPOOL
1970

PREFACE.

" There is hardly any branch of ethnology where so much remains to be done, and where the opportunities for research are so rapidly vanishing beyond recall, as the study of comparative music." When C. S. Myers wrote this in 1907, little systematic work had been attempted, and the phonograph archives at Paris, Berlin, and Vienna had not long been formed, but there seemed every hope that a subject so bound up with social anthropology in general would receive the special treatment it deserved. So far as Africa is concerned, however, the position thirty years later is little better. Such evidence as exists is scattered in travel books, ethnographical monographs and periodicals, and the note-books of explorers, missionaries and musicians. The most ambitious attempt to collect the material, H. Endo's " Bibliography of Oriental and Primitive Music ", (1929), deals only partly with Africa, and is incomplete in bibliographical detail. Apart from the excellent record of contemporary work given in each number of the Zeitschrift für Vergleichende Musikwissenschaft (1933-) and one or two general lists on anthropology and on music, there is no guide to a mass of evidence which at its best is invaluable and at its worst at least interesting. The present bibliography is an attempt to fill this gap.

Considering the incidence of music in African life, it is at first sight remarkable to find such a paucity of scientific research on the subject. One has only to glance at some such record of social custom as Van Warmelo's " Contribution towards Venda history " (1932) to be convinced of the part which music plays, not as entertainment, but as an integral part of tribal ritual. Perhaps it is this very ubiquity which has led to neglect ; musical instruments, tangible signs of æsthetic, have been better served by students of material culture than the music they produce. But there are other reasons : few explorers have been musicians and fewer musicians explorers ; the technique of recording has only recently reached a standard which could be called satisfactory, and many travellers have relied on memory, fancy and adjectival comment, with results which are anything but scientific. A few bold spirits attempted to record music by means of notation, but most of these have fallen into the temptation of harmonising it according to the fashion of their time. Some witnesses, imbued with an unenlightened missionary spirit, believed native culture to be inherently worthless and bestial, and shaped their judgments accordingly. There were those who, like Bowdich, could only hear " charming asses' music " ; others, expecting less and perceiving more, found a lively and unrivalled sense of polyphonic rhythm, the elements of melody, and what seemed an unexpected ability to improvise.

The evidence as a whole falls into several categories. Firstly, that of the early travellers. Vasco da Gama, for instance, records that on first landing at the Cape in 1497 he was greeted by a party of Hottentots playing flutes. The evidence of Dos Santos, Simon van der Stel and Tachard in South Africa, and Bosman, Merolla da Sorrarto and Montecucculo on the West Coast, is equally valuable, and it is this chance recording of instruments and music which may well have vanished subsequently that is perhaps as important as the more accurate description of later observers. Professor Kirby has already worked upon the earlier evidence of South African native music, but much remains to be done with material from other parts of the continent.

Secondly there is the evidence of missionaries, who by reason of their close contact with the natives have had unique chances of observation. There is unexpected material, for instance, in some of the dictionaries of native languages, and while one group of well meaning workers has attempted to impose a European cast on native singing, another group from Missionar Witte to the Rev. A. M. Jones has collected important evidence and attempted to work out a logical compromise which takes into account native tone-values, form and rhythm. One section* of this bibliography is intended to illustrate the work which has been done in this direction.

The work of trained anthropologists such as Rattray and Roscoe is better known ; on the whole this evidence is precise and useful, but most anthropologists apologise for their lack of musicianship, and turn over their phonograph recordings and notes to acoustic experts and analysts, by whom some of the most valuable work on the subject has so far been done. It is only necessary to mention the late Professor Erich von Hornbostel's analysis of the music of the Fang, Wanyamwezi and other tribes, to indicate the quality of this contribution to comparative musicology. Defects in methods of recording and lack of practical background may, however, be advanced as criticisms of even the best analytical material. The ideal combination of ethnologist, field worker and musician is rare enough to be called unique, and Professor Kirby of Witwatersrand University is the only practical musician who has used his opportunities in this field. Musicians generally have neglected the subject entirely, although a few, who may perhaps be called " armchair musicians," have assembled material but have attempted little serious research. It has been left to those workers on the science of music who call themselves musicologists to sustain interest in the subject, although in comparison with the distinguished work on indigenous music achieved in America, the African aspect has hitherto scarcely been touched.

The quality of this evidence is uneven, and much of it needs to be sifted and checked by comparison with the music as it now exists. This is by no means an easy matter ; musical instruments migrate, are borrowed, imitated and improved upon, and so are musical forms. The problem of provenience is complicated at the best, and the ethnologist of the future, as Professor Kirby points out, must be a historian and a linguist as well. Methods of recording are continually being

---

* African Music and the Church.

improved, opportunities of accomplishing comparative work are increasing, and at the same time the chances of discovering music in its primitive form are rapidly diminishing. Sir H. H. Johnston believed that " Music is one of the many arts in which the Negro has degenerated since the coming of the white men." So far as Southern Africa is concerned, this opinion is echoed by Professor Kirby. What is most needed at the moment, perhaps, is a dispassionate survey of the evidence that exists, good, bad and indifferent ; a checking up on authorities ; and the collection of such phonograph recordings as exist, with re-recording of earlier records if necessary. In this connection it may perhaps be pointed out that although the French and Germans made full use of their colonial opportunities in this respect, there are no central archives in England where records may be examined and worked upon ; the lack of such a resource, considering the part played by England in the administration of her African colonies is a reproach which one wishes might soon be removed.

Another section of this bibliography deals with the related question of African music in the New World. Not the least effective result of the Atlantic slave trade has been the spreading of certain patterns of thought and custom not only in Africa itself but in the Americas, North and South, and in the West Indies. So far as the music of the United States Negroes is concerned, much has been written by both the friends and the enemies of the African. In 1890, Wallaschek declared that " Spirituals are mere imitations of European compositions which the Negroes have picked up and served again with slight variations " ; and a vigorous controversy ensued which still intermittently rages. Few knowledgeable people dispute that the contribution of rhythmic devices, of the elaboration of melodic patterns, and of an unmistakeable vocal intensity, to American Negro music, is due to African origins ; the rest is anything but silence, but one might note that the question of provenience is best judged by those few with direct acquaintance with the music of both continents. This section of the Bibliography is designed only to illustrate this controversial question : the wider aspects of Negro folk music are adequately dealt with in the Survey drawn up by Dr. George Herzog*, in White's " American Negro Folk Songs " (with bibliography), and elsewhere.

The evidence concerning African music in the rest of the New World is scanty, and much work remains to be done, not only in the Guianas, Brazil and the islands, but also in the countries of Central America. The achievements of Professor Herskovits and Dr. Herzog, both of whom have worked in Africa, are an indication of the problems of comparative research which remain to be solved.

A further section of this Bibliography deals with Drum Language, a subject which, owing largely to the work of Christaller and Rattray, has been comparatively adequately treated. Other sections deal with the technique of recording and its limitations, the approach and tactful handling of natives, and the arrangement and classification of instruments, an aspect of primitive music which has been well explored by Curt Sachs and other experts.

---

* Research in primitive music and folk music in the U.S., 1936.

In his " Life of a South African tribe ", H. A. Junod remarks that " the black race is essentially musical ; its gifts in this domain are real and if properly developed will certainly produce remarkable results in time ". It is this aspect of the question which it is perhaps essential to emphasise ; African music must not be looked upon, as one writer puts it, " as a museum exhibit ", but as " a living art, capable of expressing the feelings of a living African people ". Whether it can preserve its individuality, whether it must blend in some way with European musical styles, whether music which, in South Africa, is found to have reached a stage of our own mediæval *organum* can, by the establishment of native schools of music, be developed at its own rate and in its own way ; these are problems which raise fundamental issues and which must be faced by students both of music and of sociology. They are of equal importance to the missionary and the teacher, and are symptomatic of the whole question of culture contact, since native music is a living strain in the *mores* of the African people.

INDEX.

LIST OF ABBREVIATIONS

Abh. Hamburger Kol. Inst.	Abhandlungen des Hamburger Kolonial Instituts
Acad., Akad.	Academy, Académie, Akademie, etc.
Afr.	Africa, African
Akad. Wiss. in Wien, phil. hist. Klasse	Akademie der Wissenschaften in Wien, philosophisch-historische Klasse
Allg. Musik. Zeit.	Allgemeine Musikalische Zeitung, Leipzig
Amer.	American
Amer. Acad. Polit. Soc. Sci.	American Academy of Political and Social Science, Philadelphia
Amer. Anthrop.	American Anthropologist, Washington
Amer. Jour. Psychol. ...	American Journal of Psychology, Baltimore
Amer. Jour. Sociol. ...	American Journal of Sociology, Chicago
Ann. Mus. Congo Belge ...	Annales du Musée du Congo Belge, Tervueren
Ann. Natal Mus.	Annals of the Natal Museum, Pietermaritzburg
Ann. S. Afr. Mus. ...	Annals of the South African Museum, Cape Town
Anthrop. Ser.	Anthropological Series
Archiv. Antrop. Etnol ...	Archivio per l'Antropologia e la Etnologia, Firenze
Archiv f. Anthrop. ...	Archiv für Anthropologie, Braunschweig
Archiv. Suisses Anthrop. Générale	Archives Suisses d'Anthropologie Générale, Genève
B.E.	British Empire
Bantu Stud.	Bantu Studies, Cape Town
Beitr. Kol. Polit.	Beiträge zur Kolonialpolitik, Frankfurt-a-M.
Belg. Col.	La Belgique Coloniale, Bruxelles
Berl.	Berlin
Bibl. Afr.	Bibliotheca Africana, Innsbruck
bibliog.	bibliography
Bol. Soc. Estudos Moçambique	Boletim da Sociedade de Estudos da Colonia de Moçambique, Lourenço Marques
Bol. Soc. Geog. Lisboa ...	Boletim da Sociedade de Geografia de Lisboa

Brit. Jour. Psychol., genl. sect.	British Journal of Psychology, general section
Bul. Acad. Sci. Cracovie ...	Bulletin de l'Académie de Sciences, Cracovie
Bul. Ag. Génl. Col. ...	Bulletin de l'Agence Générale des Colonies, Paris
Bul. Mus. Ethnog. Troc. ...	Bulletin du Musée d'Ethnographie du Trocadéro, Paris
Bul. Com. Etud. A.O.F. ...	Bulletin du Comité d'Etudes Historiques et Scientifiques de l'Afrique Occidentale Française, Paris
Bul. Soc. Anthrop. Paris ...	Bulletin de la Société d'Anthropologie, Paris
Bul. Soc. Rech. Cong. ...	Bulletin de la Société des Recherches Congolaises, Bruxelles
Camb.	Cambridge
Camb. Archaeol. Ethnog. Ser.	Cambridge Archaeological and Ethnographical Series
Cent. Afr.	Central Africa
Coll. Mon. Ethnog. ...	Collection de Monographies Ethnographiques, Bruxelles
Com. Afr. Franc.	Comité de l'Afrique Française
descr.	describes, description
Deut. Kol. Zeit.	Deutsche Kolonialzeitung, Berlin
Erganz.	Erganzungsheft
Ethnol. Notizblatt ...	Ethnologisches Notizblatt, Berlin
f.	für
Folk Song Soc. N.E. ...	Bulletin of the Folk Song Society of the North East, Cambridge, Mass.
Geog. Jour.	Geographical Journal
G. C. Rev.	Gold Coast Review, Accra
Harvard Afr. Stud. ...	Harvard African Studies, Cambridge, Mass.
i., illust.	illustrations, illustrated
Illust. Lond. News ...	Illustrated London News
instr.	instrument, instruments
Intern. Archiv Ethnog. ...	Internationales Archiv für Ethnographie, Leiden
Intern. Inst. Afr. Langs. & Cult.	International Institute of African Languages & Cultures
Intern. Rev. Miss. ...	International Review of Missions

Jahr. Verh. Erdk. Dres. ...	Jahresbericht des Vereins für Erdkunde, Dresden
Jahrb. Städt. Mus. Völk.	Jahrbuch des Städtischen Museums für Völkerkunde, Leipzig
Jour. Afr. Soc.	Journal of the [Royal] African Society
Jour. Amer. Folklore ...	Journal of American Folklore, New York
Jour. Manch. Geog. Soc. ...	Journal of the Manchester Geographical Society
Jour. R. Geog. Soc. ...	Journal of the Royal Geographical Society
Jour. Soc. Américanistes ...	Journal de la Société des Américanistes, Paris
Kol. Rund.	Koloniale Rundschau, Berlin
L'Anthrop.	L'Anthropologie, Paris
La Géog.	La Géographie, Paris
Leip.	Leipzig
m.	map, maps
Mag.	Magazine
Mitt.	Mitteilungen
Mitt. Anthrop. Gesell. Wien	Mitteilungen der Anthropologischen Gesellschaft, Wien
Mitt. Geog. Gesell. Hamburg	Mitteilungen der Geographischen Gesellschaft, Hamburg
Mitt. Schutz.	Mitteilungen aus den Deutschen Schutzgebieten, Berlin
Mitt. Sem. Orient. Sprach. Afr. Stud.	Mitteilungen des Seminars für Orientalische Sprachen : Afrikanische Studien, Berlin
Monatsbl. Nordd. Miss. Gesell.	Monatsblatt der Norddeutschen Missionsgesellschaft, Bremen
Mouvements Sociol. Internat.	Mouvements Sociologiques Internationaux, Bruxelles
Mus.	Museum
Mus. Jour. Phil.	Museum Journal, Philadelphia
Music. America	Musical America, New York
Music. Courier	Musical Courier, Boston
Music. Quart.	Musical Quarterly, New York
Music. Observ.	Musical Observer, New York
Musik. Wochenbl.	Musikalisches Wochenblatt, Leipzig
Nat. Geog. Mag.	National Geographical Magazine, Washington
Nat. Hist.	Natural History, New York
Neue Allg. Miss.	Neue Allgemeine Missionszeitschrift, Berlin

Oversea Educ.	Oversea Education	
Oxf.	Oxford	

Poly. Soc. ... ... Journal of the Polynesian Society, Wellington, N.Z.
phonog. ... ... phonograph
Pro. Music Teachers' Nat. Assn. ... ... Proceedings of the Music Teachers' National Association
Publ. ... ... Published, publication

R. Anthrop. Inst. ... ... Journal of the Royal Anthropological Institute
R. Soc. Geog. Ital. ... Bollettino della Reale Società Geografica Italiana, Roma
Rens. Col. ... ... Renseignements Coloniaux, Paris
Rept. Brit. Assn. ... Report of the British Association for the Advancement of Science
Rev. Anthrop. ... ... Revue d'Anthropologie, Paris
Rev. Cong. ... ... Revue Congolaise, Bruxelles
Rev. Ethnog. ... ... Revue d'Ethnographie, Paris
Rev. Ethnog. Trad. Pop. ... Revue d'Ethnographie et Traditions Populaires, Paris
Rev. Etud. Ethnog. Sociol. Revue d'Etudes ethnographiques et sociologiques, Paris
Rev. Madag. ... ... Revue de Madagascar, Antananarivo
Rev. Music ... ... La Revue Musicale, Paris
Riv. Col. Ital. ... ... Rivista delle Colonie Italiane, Roma
Riv. Mus. Ital. ... ... Rivista Musicale Italiana, Torino

S. Afr. Assn. Adv. Sci. ... Report of the South African Association for the Advancement of Science, Cape Town
S. Afr. Jour. Sci. ... ... South African Journal of Science, Cape Town
S. Afr. Rlys. Mag. ... ... South African Railways Magazine, Johannesburg
S.I.M. ... ... Société International de Musicologie, Paris
Samm. Gemein. Wiss. Vorträge ... ... Sammlung gemeinverständlicher wissenschaftlicher Vorträge
Sch. Orient. Stud. ... ... Bulletin of the School of Oriental Studies
Sitz. ... ... Sitzungsberichte
Smiths. Inst. ... ... Report of the Smithsonian Institution, Washington
Soc. Anthrop. de Bruxelles Bulletin de la Société d'Anthropologie de Bruxelles
Soc. Anthrop. de Paris ... Bulletin de la Société d'Anthropologie de Paris

Soc. des Miss. Evang. ...	Société des Missions Evangéliques, Paris
Soc. d'Editions Géog., Marit. et. Col.	Société d'Editions Géographiques, Maritimes et Coloniales, Paris
Soc. Géog. Alger	Bulletin de la Société de Géographie d'Alger
Soc. Neuchât. Géog. ...	Bulletin de la Société Neuchâteloise de Géographie
Soc. R. Belge Géog. ...	Bulletin de la Société Royale Belge de Géographie, Bruxelles
Soc. Rom. Antrop.	Atti della Società Romana di Antropologia, Roma
Soc. Sult. Géog.	Bulletin de la Société Sultanieh de Géographie, Cairo
S. Afr.	South Africa
S. Workman	Southern Workman, Hampton, Va.
Trans. Ethnol. Soc. ...	Transactions of the Ethnological Society
Trav. Mém. Inst. Ethnol.	Travaux et Mémoires de l'Institut d'Ethnologie, Paris
U.P.	University Press
U.S. Nat. Mus. Bul. ...	Bulletin of the United States National Museum, Washington
Verh. f. Naturf. Gesell. ...	Verhandlungen für Naturforschende Gesellschaft
Veröff. Mus. Völk. ...	Veröffentlichen des Museums für Völkerkunde
Veröff. Städt. Völkermus. Frankfurt-a.M.	Veröffentlichen des Städtischen Völkermuseums, Frankfurt-am-Main
W. Afr. Rev.	West African Review, Liverpool
Wash.	Washington
Zeit. f. Eingeborenen-sprachen	Zeitschrift für Eingeborenensprachen, Berlin
Zeit. f. Ethnol.	Zeitschrift für Ethnologie, Berlin
Zeit. f. Musikwiss.	Zeitschrift für Musikwissenschaft, Leipzig
Zeit. f. Vergleich. Musikwiss.	Zeitschrift für Vergleichende Musikwissenschaft, Berlin
Zeit. Intern. Musikgesell. ...	Zeitschrift der Internationalen Musikgesellschaft

I—NATIVE MUSIC IN AFRICA GENERALLY

DAPPER, OLFERT. Naukeurige Beschrijvinge der Afrikanische
Gewesten. pp.34, 112, 122, 157, 255, 259, 277. Amsterdam :
Meurs. 1676. *i.*
Collection of early references to music in several parts of Afr.

MICHAELIS, C. F. Über die Musik wilder und halbcultivierter Völker
[Allg. Musik. Zeit., 31 : 509–15, 524–30 : 1814]
*Notes on music of W. Afr., Madagascar, Hottentots, compiled
from Lichtenstein, Le Vaillant & other travellers.*

AMBROS, AUGUST WILHELM. Geschichte der Musik. *v.1, pp.11–16.*
Breslau : Leuckart. 1862.
*Secondary source : remarks on music of several tribes, with
notation.*

ENGEL, CARL. The music of the most ancient nations. *pp.10–16,*
166, 211. Murray (*reissued by Reeves, 1929*). 1864.
Gives scales of several African instr.

WOOD, J. G. Natural history of man. *v.1.* Routledge. 1868. *i.*
*Includes many references to music and instr. of Afr. tribes, compiled
from books of travels ; interesting but uncritical.*

ROWBOTHAM, JOHN FREDERICK. History of music. *pp.1–151.*
Trübner. 1885.
On primitive music : with incidental references to Afr.

ANON. Die Musik bei den afrikanischen Naturvölkern [Neue Musik-
zeitung, Köln, 7 : 181–82, 209–10 : 1886] *i.*
General (secondary) remarks on music and instruments.

BROWN, MARY ELIZABETH & ADAMS, WILLIAM. Musical instruments
& their homes. *pp.227–72.* N.Y. : Dodd, Mead. 1888.
*Deals with primitive music, & Afr. singing & instruments :
quotations from Schweinfurth, Burton, etc.*

WALLASCHEK, RICHARD. Primitive music. 326*pp.* Longmans. 1893.
bibliog. 29*pp.*
*The first ambitious attempt to collate information from travels and
similar sources : with notation.*

GROSSE, ERNST. Die Anfänge der Kunst. *pp.265–90.* Freiburg
i.B. : Siebeck. 1894.
„ The beginnings of art. *pp.278–304.* N.Y. : Appleton. 1897.
Includes chapters on the origins of music and dancing.

SCHURTZ, HEINRICH. Urgeschichte der Kultur. *pp.505–33.* Leip. :
Bibliographisches Institut. 1900. *i.*
*Notes on primitive music, instr. & dancing, with notation from
Dybowski, etc.*

COLERIDGE-TAYLOR, SAMUEL. Twenty-four negro melodies. 127*pp*.
Boston : Ditson. 1905.
*Contains notation of airs from Junod & Krehbiel (q.v.),
'harmonised'.*

C., J. L'aède antique et le griot africain [Rev. Music., 6 : 340–43 :
1906] *i*.
General remarks on professional musicians.

WORK, MONROE NATHAN. Some parallelisms in the development of
Africans & other races [S. Workman ; 36 : 106–11 : 1907]
Secondary account of instr. & songs from Wallaschek, etc.

PASTOR, WILLY. Die Musik der Naturvölker und die Anfänge der
europäischer Musik. 1 : Die Naturvölker [Zeit. f. Ethnol., 42 :
654–64 : 1910]

„ *Ditto, translated.* The music of primitive peoples & the beginnings
of European music [Smiths. Inst., Wash., 1912 : 697–88, 1912]
*General discussion of part played by percussion in primitive music,
origins of instr., & music as ' rhythm, magic & melody '.*

SCHMIDT, WILHELM. Die Stellung der Pygmaenvölker in der Entwick-
lungsgeschichte des Menschen. *pp*.128–31. Stuttgart : Strecker.
1910.
Instr. & singing of Pygmies descr.

HORNBOSTEL, ERICH M. von. Musik der Naturvölker. *In* MEYER :
Grosses Konversations-Lexikon. *v*.24, *pp*.638–43. Leip. : Bibliographisches Institut. 1911–12 (Supplt.)
*Notes on Afr. music, with notation of Mashona & Fang melodies
from phonog. recordings.*

STUMPF, CARL. Die Anfänge der Musik. 209*pp*. Leip. : Barth.
1911. *i*.
A suggestive treatise on the origins of music ; see especially pt.2 :
Gesänge der Naturvölker, *with notation of many airs from phonog.
records, & illust. of instr.*

BINGHAM, W. V. Five years of progress in comparative musical science
[Psychological Bulletin, Lancaster, Pa., 11 : 421–33 : 1914]
*Includes survey of work done on Afr. music, with four-page
bibliography.*

McCULLOCH, JOHN ARNOTT. Music, primitive & savage. *In* Encyclo-
pædia of Religion & Ethics, ed. James Hastings. *v*.9, *pp*.5–10.
Clark. 1917. *bibliog*.
*Compact survey of primitive music including Afr., with notes on
its social significance.*

CURTIS, NATALIE BURLIN. Songs & tales from the Dark Continent.
pp.xix–xxiii. N.Y. : Schirmer. [1920]
*Describes songs, singing & general merits of Afr. music : see also
Portuguese E. Afr. and S. Afr.*

HORNBOSTEL, ERICH M. von. Musik der Eingeborenen. *In* Deutsches
Kolonial Lexikon, ed. Heinrich Schnee. *v*.2, *pp*.602–05. Leip. :
Quelle. 1920. *i*.
*Notes on Afr. music & instr. with notation of airs from Togo,
Kamerun & E. Afr. See also pp*.454–55 & *v*.3, *pp*.458–59.

Huot, Louis. L'âme noire : l'homme primitif centre africain [Mercure de France, Paris, 151 : 387–90 : 1921]
Brief account of Afr. ' musical sense '.

Buschan, Georg, ed. Illustrierte Völkerkunde. *v.*1, *pp.*470, 486, 515–16, 529, 537, 550, 557, 563, 586, 597, 604, 609. Stuttgart : Strecker. 1922. *i.*
Brief notes on music of many tribes.

Hare, Maud Cuney. Africa in song [Metronome, N.Y., 38/9 : 157–58 ; /10 : 80–81 ; /12 : 60–62 : 1922]
Compilation of earlier references to songs & singing, with notation from Junod & others.

Tiersot, Julien. La musique chez les nègres d'Afrique. *In* Encyclopédie de la musique et dictionnaire du Conservatoire, ed. Lavignac. *v.*5, *pt.*1, *pp.*3197–3225. Paris. 1922. *i.*
Summary of data concerning music of the Nile Basin, W. Afr., S. Afr., & Madagascar : with many musical illustrations.

Frobenius, Leo. Das sterbende Afrika. *pp.*72–75. München : O.C. Recht Verlag. 1923. *i.*
Somewhat rhetorical account of music & dancing.

Anon. Ein Klavier für afrikanische Musik [Der Kolonialdeutsche, Berl., 4 : 197 : 1924]
Brief note on Ballanta's projected seventeen-tone piano.

Lyle, Watson. Negermusik [Auftakt, Prague, 5 : 15–16 : 1925]
Very general account of Afr. music.

Hambly, Wilfrid Dyson. Tribal dancing & social development. 296*pp.* Witherby. 1926. *i. bibliog.* 11*pp.*
By the Assistant Curator of the Afr. Department, Field Museum, Chicago ; assembling much data about instr., singing & dancing.

Kappe, G. Tanz und Trommel der Neger. *In* Festschrift zum 70 Geburtstag von H. H. Schauinsland. *pp.*64–67. Bremen. 1927.
Discusses relationship between music, drum-rhythms & dancing.

Weber, Wolfgang. Negermusik : eine Urform der Unsrigen ? [Die Musik, Berl., 19 : 697–702 : 1927] *i.*
Popular account of melody, rhythm, harmony, with notation of Wadschagga songs.

Hornbostel, Erich M. von. African music [Africa, 1 : 30–62 : 1928]
,, Ditto. 35*pp.* London : Intern. Inst. Afr. Langs. & Cults. 1928.
A compact and authoritative statement of present knowledge concerning African music : important and suggestive.

Pritchard, E. E. Evans. The dance [Africa, 1 : 447–53 : 1928]
General account of the dance, with incidental reference to music.

Rühl, Th. African negro music [Anthropos, Wien, 23 : 684–85 : 1928] *Review of* Hornbostel : African Music ; *discusses possible developments of Afr. music.*

Weber, Wolfgang. Was ist Negermusik ? [Velhagen & Klasings Monatshefte, Bielefeld, 42 : 566–70 : 1928] *i.*
A popular introductory article.

CHAUVET, STEPHEN. Musique nègre. 242*pp.* Paris : Soc. d'Editions Géog., Marit. et Col. 1929. *i. bibliog.* 2*pp.*
>   *Full but not always accurate treatment of music & instr., song & dance, largely derivative : with good plates, & notation.*

LACHMANN, ROBERT. Die Musik der aussereuropäischer Natur- und Kulturvölker [Handbuch der Musikwissenschaft, 35] 33*pp.* Potsdam : Wild Park. 1929.
>   *pp.1–16 deals with the melody, rhythms & form of Afr. music.*

LAVAUDEN, THÉRÈSE. African orchestics [Chesterian, 10 : 127–33 : 1929]

,, Orchestique africaine [Le Guide Musical, Paris, 3 : 230–33 : 1930]
>   *Discussion on psychological effects of music & dancing of the Negro and their supposed relationship with jazz.*

SCHILDE, WILLY. Die afrikanischen Hochzeitszeichen [Zeit. f. Ethnol., 61 : 117–24 : 1929] *bibliog.* 9*pp.*
>   *Describes the social significance of Afr. music & instr.*

JUNK, VIKTOR. Handbuch des Tanzes. 264*pp.* Stuttgart : Klett. 1930. *See* chapters on Afrikanische Tanze & Musikbegleitung zum Tanz.

SACHS, CURT. Vergleichende Musikwissenschaft in ihren Grundzugen. 87*pp. bibliog.* Leip. : Quelle. 1930.
>   *A good account of the theory & analysis of primitive music, illust. by notation from several Afr. tribes, from phonog. recordings.*

SPENCER, HERBERT. Descriptive sociology, or groups of sociological facts classified & arranged by H.S. No. 4 : African races, ed. by E. Torday. *pp.*371–82. Williams & Norgate. 1930.
>   *Short extracts on music & instr. from many authorities, arranged according to tribal groups.*

BUCHT, L. Frau Musika bei den Eingeborenen [Jambo, Leip., 8 : 61–68 : 1931]
>   *A popular account in dialogue form.*

HEINITZ, WILHELM. Strukturprobleme in primitiver Musik. 258*pp.* Hamburg : Friederichsen. 1931. *bibliog.* 2*pp.*
>   *Deals with problems of time, rhythm, melody & tonality, with notation from music of Afr. tribes (phonog. recordings).*

HICHENS, WILLIAM. Music : a triumph of African art [Discovery, 12 : 192–95 : 1931]

,, *(Reprinted)* [Art & Archaeology, 36–41, 1932] *i.*
>   *Good short popular account of music & instr.*

WEBER, WOLFGANG. Co wiemy dziś o muzyce murzyńskiej [Muzkya, Warsaw, 8 : 459–61 : 1931]
>   *A popular account of African music.*

DUBOIS, HENRI. Le répertoire africain. *pp.*49–56. Roma : La Sodalité de St. Pierre Clavier. 1932.
>   *Informative comparison of European & Afr. music : antiphony, polyphony, rhythm & structure discussed, with additional note by Rühl.*

TRACEY, HUGH T.   African folk music [Man, 32 : 118–19 : 1932]
Note on relation between intonation & melody in Afr. folk-songs.
WATSON, JOHN T.   African music [Choir, 158–59 : 1932]
Brief popular article stressing the hiatus between European tunes & those adapted to Afr. speech tones.
AMU, E.   How to study African rhythm [Teacher's Jour., G.C., 6 : 121–24 : 1933–34]
Useful practical account by a native musician & composer.
CHAUVET, STEPHEN.   Musique et chants nègres [Visage du Monde, Paris, 4 : 78–86 : 1933]
A very general account.
LENOIR, RAYMOND.   La musique comme institution sociale [L'Anthrop., 43 : 47–81 : 1933]
Discusses place of music in tribal life.
SACHS, CURT.   Eine Weltgeschichte des Tanzes. 325pp. Berl. : Reimer. 1933. *bibliog.*
See especially pp.123–138, with notation from Hornbostel.
TANGHE, JOSEPH.   La musique nègre [La Revue Sincère, Brux., 11 274–84 : 1933]
Critique of Chauvet : Musique nègre ; discussion of rhythm,: polyphony & pentatonic scale. See also extracts in Congo, 397–403 : 1934.
TIERSOT, JULIEN.   Chansons nègres recueillies, traduites et harmonisées. Paris : Heugel. 1933.
Contains airs from several Afr. tribes.
ALAKIJA, OLUWOLE AYODELE.   Is the African musical ?   *In* Negro Anthology, ed. Nancy Cunard. pp.407–09. Wishart. 1934.
Popular account of music in Afr. life, with notation.
JONES, ARTHUR MORRIS.   African drumming [Bantu Stud., 8 : 1–16 : 1934]
Useful account by a field-worker in Rhodesia, urging the basic simplicity of Afr. polyphonic rhythm.
JOWITT, HAROLD.   Suggested methods for the African school. pp.221–27. Longmans. 1934.
Chapter on the teaching of music : advocates encouragement of dancing, drumming, local songs, tuning of instr. by ear & voice production.
SCHNEIDER, MARIUS.   Geschichte der Mehrstimmigkeit : I—Die Naturvölker. pp.15–30, 65–106, & 24 pages of notation. Berl. : Bard. 1934.
Full discussion by the Director of the Berl. Phonogrammarchiv. on melody, tone, polyphony & harmony, with 165 music examples.
KNOSP, GASTON.   La melodie nègre. *In* Cinquante années d'activité coloniale au Congo, 1885–1935. pp.298–99. Brux. : L'Avenir Belge. 1935.
A general account of Afr. melody.
MACKENZIE, Mrs. D. R.   African music [Books for Africa, 6 : 35–37 : 1936]
A brief account of teaching experience in E. Africa.

II—NATIVE MUSICAL INSTRUMENTS IN AFRICA GENERALLY

BONANNI, FILIPPO. Gabinetto armonico. *pp.*117–18, 128, 153–54, 156, 174–75, 176. Roma : Placho. 1722. *i.*
> *Interesting plates & good descriptions of several instr.*

COMETTANT, JEAN PIERRE OSCAR. La musique, les musiciens et les instr. de musique, chez les différents peuples du monde. *pp.*525–29. Paris : Lévy. 1869. *i.*
> *Brief notes on several instr.*

HARTMANN, ROBERT. Die Völker Afrikas. *pp.*193–202. Leip. : Brockhaus. 1879. *i.*
> *Brief description of Afr. instr. & their distribution.*

ELSON, LOUIS C. Curiosities of music. *pp.*251–79. Boston : Ditson. 1880.
> *Notes on instr., compiled from Schweinfurth, Speke, Baker, Stanley & other travellers.*

BROWN, MARY ELIZABETH & ADAMS, WILLIAM. Musical instr. & their homes. *pp.*227–72. N.Y. : Dodd, Mead. 1888.
> *Deals with primitive music, & Afr. singing & instr. : quotations from Schweinfurth, Burton, etc.*

MASON, OTIS T. Geographical distribution of the musical bow [Amer. Anthrop., 10 : 377–80 : 1897]
> *Including description & location of ten Afr. bows.*

FROBENIUS, LEO. Der Ursprung der Kultur. *pp.*118–93. Berl. : Borntraeger. 1898. *m. & i.*
> *Enumerates Afr. instr. & their distribution according to the author's Kulturkreis theory : with classification.*

WALLASCHEK, RICHARD. Urgeschichte der Saiteninstrumente [Mitt. Anthrop. Gesell. Wien, 28 : (1)–(5) : 1898]
> *General remarks on evolution of stringed instr., with Afr. examples.*

BALFOUR, HENRY. The natural history of the musical bow. 87*pp.* Oxf. : Clarendon Press. 1899. *m. & i.*
> *Shows evolution & geographical distribution of the musical bow, especially in Afr.*

KRAUSE, EDOUARD. Die altesten Pauken [Globus, Braunschweig, 78 : 193–96 : 1900] *i.*
> *Describes evolution of various kettle-drums.*

ANKERMANN, BERNHARD. Die afrikanischen Musikinstrumenten [Ethnol. Notizbl., 3 : 1–134 : 1901] *m. & i.*
> *Many instr. described, classified & illust. in an attempt to trace origin & evolution. Geographical distribution shown on 3 maps.*

FROBENIUS, LEO. Die Saiteninstrumente der Naturvölker [Prometheus, Berl., 12 : 648–52 : 1901]
> *Notes on Afr. stringed instr.*

ROSE, ALGERNON S. Afr. primitive instr. [Pro. Music. Assn., 30 : 91–108 : 1904]
> *General description of many instr.*

ANKERMANN, BERNHARD. Kulturkreise in Afrika [Zeit. f. Ethnol., 37 : 68–69 : 1905] *m*.
Note on distribution of instr.

,, Über den gegenwärtigen Stand der Ethnographie der Südhälfte Afrikas [Archiv f. Anthrop., 32 : 274–75 : 1905]
Notes on distribution of instr.

,, L'ethnographie actuel de l'Afrique meridionale. Pt. 7 : La musique [Anthropos, Wien, 1 : 926–28 : 1906] *m*.
Showing distribution & migration of sansa, lyre, panpipes & other instr.

BALFOUR, HENRY. The friction drum [R. Anthrop. Inst., 37 : 67–92 : 1907] *i*.
Origin of Afr. friction drum traced to the smith's bellows : geographical distribution & description given.

BAGLIONI, S. Contributo alla conoscenza della musica naturale [Soc. Rom. Antrop., 15 : 313–60 : 1910]

,, *Ditto : translated into German.* [Globus, Braunschweig, 98 : 232–36, 249–54, 264–68 : 1910]
Examines acoustics & range of marimbas, sansas & panpipes, to discover ' basic physio-psychology of musical aesthetics common to all men '.

SACHS, CURT. Real-Lexicon der Musikinstrumente. xvii.442*pp*. Berl. : Bard. 1913.
Exhaustive alphabetical list including many Afr. instr.

CRAWLEY, A. E. Drums & cymbals. *In* Encyclopaedia of Religion & Ethics, ed. James Hastings. *v*.5, *pp*.89–94. Clark. 1917.
Includes general remarks on Afr. drums.

WHEELER, ADDISON J. Gongs & bells. *In* Encyclopaedia of Religion & Ethics, ed. James Hastings. *v*.6, *p*.316. Clark. 1917.
Notes on Afr. gongs.

HARE, MAUD CUNEY. The drum in Africa [Music. Observ., 17/7 : 7–8 ; & 17/8 : 9 : 1918]
Secondary source : quotations from Schweinfurth, etc., etc.

LYLE, WATSON. Afr. primitive instrumental music [Fanfare, 1 : 67 : 1921]
Generalised remarks on instr.

FROBENIUS, LEO. Atlas Africanus. *Heft* 3, *Blatt* 17, *No*. 8. München : Beck. 1922. *m*.
Map showing distribution of the harp & lyre.

STRUCK, BERNHARD. Afrikanische Kugelflöten [Kol. Rund., Heft 2–6 ; 56–63, 190–200, 236–51 : 1922] *m*. & *i*.
Many examples of the globe-fruit ocarina compared, & distribution mapped.

HARE, MAUD CUNEY. How the drum was used in Africa [Metronome, N.Y. : 40/5 : 26–27, 54 : 1924]
Secondary sources : quotations from Johnston, Bowdich, etc.

PERRON, MICHEL. Instruments à percussion du son en Europe et en
A.O.F. [Bul. Com. Etud. A.O.F., 692–715 : 1924] *i.*
*Traces development of medieval ' tabours ' in Afr., describing many
drums.*

LEHMANN, JOHANNES. Beiträge zur Musikinstrumenten-Forschung.
Saiteninstr., Flöten. *In* Festschrift 25jähr. Bestehen Frankf.
gesell. Anthrop. Ethnol. Urgeschichte. *pp.*113–25. Frankfurt-a-M. :
Bechhold. 1925. *i.*
*Descr. & ill. Afr. stringed instr. & flutes in Frankfurter Völker-
museum.*

LANE, SARA. Some musical instr. of the primitive African [S. Workman,
56 : 552–56 : 1927] *i.*
Describing several instr. in the museum at Hampton Institute.

HEINITZ, WILHELM. Instrumentenkunde [Handbuch der Musikwissenschaft 4] 152*pp.* Potsdam : Wild Park. 1928. *i.*
*See index : Afrika, & under names of separate instr., each of which
is treated historically.*

SACHS, CURT. Der Ursprung der Saiteninstrumente. *In* Festschrift :
publication d'hommage offerte au P. W. Schmidt, ed. W. Koppers.
*pp.*629–34. Wien : Mechitharisten-Congregations-Buchdruckerei.
1928.
Describes evolution of stringed instruments.

CHAUVET, STEPHEN. Musique nègre. 242*pp.* Paris : Soc. d'Editions
Géog., Marit. et Col. 1929. *i. bibliog.* 2*pp.*
Description & good illust. of many instr.

CRAWLEY, ERNEST. Dress, drink & drums. *pp.*233–62. Methuen.
1931. *i.*
*General remarks on the art & psychology of drumming, describing
various types of drum.*

NADEL, SIEGFRIED F. Marimba-musik [Akad. Wiss. in Wien, phil.-hist.
Klasse, Sitz. 212] 63*pp.* Wien. 1931. *m. & i.*
*Many types of Afr. marimba descr. & distribution shown : examines
tone, range & frequency, & analyses several phonog. records.*

MONTANDON, GEORGE. Nouveaux exemplaires africains de la cithare
en radeau [L'Anthrop., 42 : 676–78 : 1932] *i.*
A discussion of Afr. sansas.

NADEL, SIEGFRIED F. Zur Ethnographie des afrikanischen Xylophons
[Forschungen & Fortschritte, Leip., 444–45 : 1932] *m.*
Short note on dispersion of xylo, with descr. of several types.

HORNBOSTEL, ERICH M. von. The ethnology of African sound instr .
[Africa, 5 : 129–54, 277–311 : 1933]
*Important attempt to group African instr. in relation to their
extra-Afr. distribution : with glossary.*

WIESCHHOFF, HEINZ. Die afrikanischen Trommeln und ihre ausser-
afrikanischen Beziehungen. 148*pp.* Stuttgart : Strecker. 1933.
m. & i. bibliog. 10*pp.*
*Construction, manner of playing, & musical & social significance
of many drums described.*

KIRBY, PERCIVAL R. Reed-flute ensembles of South Africa [R. Anthrop. Inst., 63 : 313-88 : 1933] *i.*
> *Exhaustive collation of data regarding construction, use & technical detail of reed-flutes : well illust. (see plates 18–26)*

„ Musical instr. of the native races of South Africa. 296*pp.* Milford. 1934. *m. & i.*
> *An intensive study of the evolution, construction, playing & tribal significance of 100 instr., with musical notation & many plates.*

„ Note on Hornbostel : The ethnology of African sound instr. [Africa, 7 : 107–09 : 1934]
> *Note on origin of sansa.*

TRACEY, HUGH T. The tuning of musical instr. [Nada, Bulawayo, 13 : 35–44 : 1935] *i.*
> *Detailed descr. of Mashona methods of tuning a sansa.*

KUNST, JAAP. Ein musikologischer Beweis für Kulturzusammenhänge zwischen Indonesien—vermutlich Java—und Zentralafrika [Anthropos, Wien, 31 : 131–40 : 1936] *i.*
> *Comparison of frequencies & performance-qualities of marimbas from Central Africa & the East.*

III—NATIVE MUSIC IN AFRICA—SPECIFIC COUNTRIES

1—SOMALILAND

REINISCH, LEO. Der Dschäbärtidialekt der Somalisprache [Akad. Wiss. in Wien, phil.-hist. Klasse, Sitz., 148, *pp.*107–08, 1848]
> *Gives notation of marriage-song & lullaby.*

RÉVOIL, GEORGES. La vallée du Darror. *pp.*335–36. Paris : Challamel. 1882.
> *Includes notation of war-song.*

PAULITSCHKE, PHILIPP VIKTOR. Ethnographie nordost-afrikas. *v.*1, *pp.*148,250–51, *v.*2, *pp.*217–21. Berl. : Reimer. 1893.
> *Notes on Somali music, with notation.*

PESENTI, GUSTAVO. Canti e ritmi arabici, somalici e swahili [R. Soc. Geog. Ital., 47 : 1409–32 : 1910]
> *Contains notation of many airs, chiefly Arabian in character.*

„ Di alcuni canti arabici e somalici [R. Soc. Geog. Ital., 49 : 58–63 : 1912]
> *Gives notation of five songs of Arabian character.*

HEINITZ, WILHELM. Über die Musik der Somali [Zeit. f. Musikwiss., 2 : 257–63 : 1920]
> *Describing the drum, songs & dances of the Somali, with notation of nine songs from phonog. recordings.*

ELLIOTT, J. A. G. A visit to the Bajun islands [Jour. Afr. Soc., 25 : 247 & note : 1925]
> *Wind instr. & percussion instr. described.*

BARDI, BENNO. Stimmaufnahmen bei den Somal [Signale für die Musikalische Welt., Berl., 84 : 469–70 : 1926–27]
Short note on effect of European music on Somalis.

CARAVAGLIOS, G. Per lo studio della musica indigena nelle nostre colonie [Riv. Col. Ital., 8 : 937–46 : 1934]
Urges scientific study of music through field-work.

2—ABYSSINIA

LOBO, JERONYMO. Voyage historique d'Abissinie. *p.*78. Paris : Gosse. 1728.

„ Voyage to Abyssinia [Pinkerton's voyages, 15 : 27 : 1814].
Note on instr.

SALT, HENRY. Voyage to Abyssinia, 1809–10. *pp.*380–81, 447. Rivington. 1814.
Brief account of instr.

LEFEBVRE, THÉOPHILE. Voyage en Abyssinie : v.1—Relation historique. *pp.*lxviii–lxx, 300–01. Paris : Bertrand. [1844–45]
Descr. several percussion instr. & dancing, with note on griots.

BENT, J. THEODORE. Sacred city of the Ethiopians. *pp.*25–29. Longmans. 1893.
Lyre, flute, trumpet & rattle descr.

PAULITSCHKE, PHILIPP VIKTOR. Ethnographie nordost-afrikas. *v.*1, *pp.*148, 250–51 : v.2, *pp.* 217–21. Berl. : Reimer. 1893–96.
Descr. singing & instr. of Danâkil & Galla, with notation (harmonised) of several airs.

VERNEAU, R. Anthropologie et ethnographie. *In* J. DUCHESNE-FOURNET : Mission en Ethiopie. *v.*2, *pp.*339–40. Paris : Masson. 1901–03.
Of little importance : brief mention of instr.

ROSEN, FELIX. Eine deutsche Gesandtschaft in Abessinien. *p.*269. Leip. : Verlag von Veit. 1907. *i.*
Note on music & instr., with illust. of Schoa lyre.

LÜPKE, THEODOR von. Profan– und Kultbauten Nordabessiniens. *In* Deutsche-Aksum Expedition. *v.*3, *p.*98. Berl. : Reimer. 1913. *i.*
Rattle, drums, flutes, lyres descr. & illust.

MONTANDON, GEORGE. Au pays Ghimirra [Soc. Neuchât. Géog., 22 : 194–95 : 1913] *i.*
Descr. trombone, globe-fruit whistle & other instr.

CASTRO, LINCOLN de. Nella terra dei Negus. *v.*1, *pp.*309–11, *et seq.* Milano : Trèves. 1915. *i.*
Flutes & lyres descr. & illust. ; see also v.2. plates xxv, xxvi.

REIN, G. K. Abessinien. *v.*3, *pp.*335–36. Berl. : Reimer. 1921. *i.*
Notes on music & instr. : see also index, v.3.

BIEBER, FRIEDRICH J. Kaffa : ein altkuschitisches Volkstum in Inner-Afrika. *v.*2, *pp.*328–34. Munster : Anthropos-Bibliothek. 1923.
Descr. singing, voice-quality, work songs & choruses.

REY, CHARLES FERNAND. Unconquered Abyssinia as it is to-day. *pp*.166–68. Seeley Service. 1923.
A popular account of instr. & music.

HEINITZ, WILHELM. Analyse eines abessinischen Harfenliedes. *In* Festschrift Meinhof. *pp*.263–74. Hamburg : Friederichsen. 1927.
Analysis of phonog. transcriptions.

RÖHRER, ERNST FRIEDRICH. Beiträge zur Kenntnis der materiellen Kultur der Amhara. *pp*.154–58 & *plate* 12. Schönberg-Bern : Wälchli. 1932.
Descr. rattle, drums & stringed instr.

HERSCHER-CLÉMENT,*** Chants d'Abyssinie [Zeit. f. Vergleich. Musikwiss., 2 : 51–57, 24*–38* : 1934]
Notes on modes & singing, with notation transcribed from records in the Sorbonne.

GRIAULE, MARCEL. Jeux et divertissements abyssins. 258*pp*. Paris : Leroux. 1935. *i.*
See index : Musique.

3—ANGLO-EGYPTIAN SUDAN

VILLOTEAU, GUILLAUME ANDRÉ. De l'état actuel de l'art musical en Egypte. *pp*.127–35. Paris : L'Imprimerie Impériale. 1812.
Descr. music & dancing of Barabras & Dongola.

MORLANG, FRANZ. Reisen östlich und westlich von Gondokoro, 1859 [Petermanns Mitt., Erganz., 2 : 119 : 1862]
Note on Bari songs & horn.

BAKER, *Sir* SAMUEL WHITE. The Albert Nyanza . . . & exploration of the Nile sources. *v.*1, *pp*.243–44. Macmillan. 1866.
Brief descr. of Lotuko funeral dance.

„ Ismailia. *v.*1, *pp.* 241–42 ; *v.*2, *p.*276. Macmillan. 1874.
Note on Bari drum & flageolet.

SCHWEINFURTH, GEORG AUGUST. Im Herzen von Afrika. *v.*1, *pp*.314–16, 421, 449–50 ; *v.*2, 81, 122, 126. Leip. : Brockhaus. 1874. *i.*

„ The heart of Africa. *v.*1, *pp*.130–33, 197–98, 293–95 ; *v.*2, *pp*.29, 58, 61, 248. Sampson Low. 1878.
Observations on music & instr. of Mittu, Bongo & Niam-Niam : with notation of a Mittu air.

„ Artes africanae. Leip. : Brockhaus. 1875. *i.*
See plates I, III, VIII, IX, XI, XIV, XVI, XVII : good illust. of Dinka drum, Bongo, Mittu, Niam-Niam and Mangbettu instr., with brief descriptive notes.

HARTMANN, R. Die Nilländer. *pp*.50, 89, 158. Leip. : Freytag. 1884.
Notes on Nubian songs & Bongo music.

ZÖLLNER, HEINRICH. Einiges über sudanesische Musik [Musik. Wochenbl., 16 : 446 : 1885]
Contains notation of three songs : descr. instr. & rhythm.

KARSTEN, PAULA. Tambura der Krieger des Mahdi (Sudanneger) [Chorgesang, Stuttgart, *No.* 24, 1889]

„ *Ditto* [Neue Musik. Rundschau, *No.* 1, 1908]

MOUNTENEY-JEPHSON, A. J. Emin Pasha & the rebellion at the Equator. *pp.*39, 106. Sampson Low. 1890.
    Brief notes on a band of drums & horns, & on Makraka instr.

CASATI, GAETANO. Zehn Jähre in Aequatoria und die Rückkeln mit Emin Pascha. *v.*1, *pp.*48, 195. Bamberg : 1891. *i.*
    Mention of Dinka feast songs & Mangbettu instr.

JUNKER, WILHELM JOHANN. Reisen in Afrika, 1875–86. *v.*1, *pp.*175, 301, 425, 434 ; *v.*3, *pp.*15–16. Wien : Hölzel. 1891. *i.*
  ,, Travels in Africa, 1875–86. *v.*1, *pp.*246–47, 354–55 ; *v.*3, *pp.*15–16. Chapman & Hall. 1890–92. *i.*
    Mention of music & instr. of various Sudanese tribes.

ANON. La musique chez les nègres [Congo Illustré, Brux., No. 6 : 48 ; No. 9 : 66–67 : 1893] *i.*
    Secondary note on singing & instr. of Azande, from Schweinwurth, etc.

FROBENIUS, HERMAN. Die Heiden-Neger des Ägyptischen Sudan. *pp.*161–72. Berl. : Reimer. 1893.
    Remarks on music, singing & instr. of Bongo, Mittu & Azande, with notation.

BURROWS, GUY. Land of Pygmies. *pp.*83–84, 183. Pearson. 1898. *i.*
    Mangbettu war drum, trumpets & bow-tapping descr.

CUMMINS, STEVENSON LYLE. Sub-tribes of Bahr-el-Ghazal Dinkas [R. Anthrop. Inst., 34 : 161–62 : 1904]
    Note on Dinka music & songs.

VAN den PLAS, J. Les Kuku [Coll. Mon. Ethnog. 6] *pp.*309–12. Brux. 1907.
    Notes on dancing, singing & instr.

MECKLENBURG, ADOLF FRIEDRICH, *Herzog* zu. Vom Kongo zum Niger und Nil. *v.*1, *p.*57 ; *v.*2, *pp.*72–73. Leip. : Brockhaus. 1912. *i.*
    Notes on Sara drums, Azande mandolin, & Mangbettu instr.

STEVENS, ETHEL STEFANA [i.e. Miss E. M. DROWER] My Sudan year. *pp.*99–114. Mills & Boon. 1912.
    Chapter on ' Sudanese songs & singers ', with incidental comment on music.

ANON. Spielleute und Märchenerzähler Innerafrikas [Westermanns Monatshefte, Braunschweig, 115 : 573–85 : 1913] *i.*
    Illust. of Sudan harps, with comments.

MEINHOF, CARL. Studienfahrt nach Kordofan [Abh. Hamburger Kol. Inst., 35] *p.*91. 1916. *i.*
    Illust. & descr. of Nuba lyre instr.

CZEKANOWSKI, JAN. Forschungen in Nil-Kongo-Zwischengebiet. *v.*6, *pt.*2, *pp.*38–40, 146–48. Leip. : Klinkhardt. 1924.
    Notes on instr. of Azande & Mangbettu.

HOFMAYR, WILHELM. Die Schilluk. *pp.*322–23, 483–90, 501–13. Wien : Anthropos-Bibliothek. 1925.
    Characteristics of Shilluk music descr. by P. Lehr : notes on instr., drum-rhythms, and notation of 16 airs (phonog.)

SELIGMAN, CHARLES GABRIEL & SELIGMAN, BRENDA Z. The social organisation of the Lotuko [Sudan Notes & Records, Khartoum, 8 : 12–14 : 1925]
>*Incidental mention of drums & drum-houses.*

BAUMANN, HERMANN. Die materielle Kultur der Azande und Mangbetu [Baessler Archiv, Leip., 11 : 63–71 : 1927]   *m. & i.*
>*Contains detailed inventory of instr., & study of their distribution & migration.*

LARKEN, P. M. Impressions of the Azande [Sudan Notes & Records, Khartoum, 10 : 103–08 : 1927]
>*Detailed descr. of drums, lutes, xylo, horns & rattle: notes on nature of songs & dancing.*

BERNATZIK, HUGO ADOLF. Zwischen Weissem Nil und Belgisch-Kongo. *Plates* 39, 40, 59–60, 73, 93–94, 106, 158, 160. Wien : Seidel. 1929. *i.*
>*Excellent illust. of Dinka, Niambara, Moru & Nuba instr. & dancing.*

PRITCHARD, E. E. EVANS. The Zande corporation of witch-doctors [R. Anthrop. Inst., 62 : 302, 315, 317–20 : 1932]
>*Observations on songs & music accompanying séances.*

ROBINSON, ARTHUR E. Sudan drums [Man, 32 : 259–61 : 1932]   *i.*
>*Nine drums & a stringed instr. descr. & illust.*

TUCKER, ARCHIBALD NORMAN. Music in S. Sudan [Man, 32 : 18–19 : 1932]
>*Note on scale of Nuer & Shilluk : descr. of instr. & their distribution.*

,, Children's games and songs in the Southern Sudan [R. Anthrop. Inst., 63 : 165–87 : 1933]   *i.*
>*Contains discussion & notation of 60 game-songs.*

,, Tribal music & dancing in S. Sudan at social & ceremonial gatherings. 57*pp.* W. Reeves. 1933. *i.*
>*Detailed study of song, dance & music of the Azande, Nuer, & Shilluk : with notation, & drum rhythms.*

4—OUBANGUI–CHARI–TCHAD.

MACKENZIE, DONALD. Flooding of the Sahara. *pp.*56–57. Sampson Low. 1877.
>*Contains brief descr. of Mandingo instr. from ' near Chad '.*

DYBOWSKI, JEAN. La route du Tchad. *pp.*198-99. Paris : Firmin-Didot. 1895. *i.*
>*Gives notation of 2 Banziri boat songs.*

REGELSPERGER, GUSTAVE. Les instr. de musique dans le pays du Chari-Tchad [La Nature, Paris, 37 : 19–22 : 1908]   *i.*
>*Useful description of Baya & Moundan instr. with illust.*

CHEVALIER, AUGUSTE. Mission Chari-Lac Tchad, 1902–04. *pp.*100–01, 149. Paris : Challamel. 1907. *i.*
>*Observations on songs, dances & instr. of the Banda.*

CARBOU, HENRI. La région du Tschadel du Ouadai. *v.*1, *pp.*71–72. Paris : Leroux. 1912.
> *Kanembu drums & bells descr.*

CUREAU, ADOLPHE. Les sociétés primitives de l'Afrique Equatoriale. *pp.*91–96. Paris : Colin. 1912.
> *Remarks on singing & dancing, with notation of two Azande airs & Bangala & Banziri boat songs.*

MacLEOD, OLIVE. Chiefs & cities of Central Africa. *pp.*20–22, 50, 230–31, 300. Edinburgh : Blackwood. 1912. *i.*
> *Notes on Garua instr., notation of boat song, note on humming.*

MECKLENBURG, ADOLF FRIEDRICH, *Herzog* zu. Vom Kongo zum Niger und Nil. *v.*1, *pp.*57. Leip. : Brockhaus. 1912. *i.*
> *Descr. of Sara drum.*

GILLIER, *Lieut.* Les Bandas : notes ethnographiques [Rens. Col., 23 : 392 : 1913]
> *Note on dances, tambourine, slit drum & xylophone.*

BRUSSEAUX, *** Note sur les Moundans [Bul. Soc. Rech. Cong., 2 : 35–37, 47 : 1922]
> *Brief notes on dancing & instr.*

GIDE, ANDRÉ. Musiques et danses au Tchad [Rev. Music., 4 : 97–100, 1927]
> *Generalised remarks on songs & dances, with notation of two melodies.*

„ Afrikanische Flussfahrt [Atlantis, Leip., 1 : 204–05 : 1929] *i.*
> *Incidental comments on songs : see good illust. of tam-tam on p.208.*

„ Travels in the Congo. *pp.*111–12, 223–26, 232–34. N.Y. : Knopf. 1930.
> *Descr. Sara chant & dancing, with attempted notation.*

DAIGRE, *Le R. P.* Les Bandas de l'Oubangui-Chari [Anthropos, Wien, 26 : 655 : 1931]
> *Descr. dances, drums, xylo, guitar, horns & flutes.*

HEINITZ, WILHELM. Eine Melodienprobe von den Sara-Kaba [Vox, Hamburg, 17 : 69–71 : 1931]
> *Contains analysis & notation from phonog. recording.*

EBOUÉ, FÉLIX. Les peuples de l'Oubangui-Chari. *pp.*75–94. Paris : Com. Afr. Franc. 1933. *i.*

„ *Ditto* [Rens. Col., 42 : 461–62 : 1932 ; 43 : 14–19 : 1933]
> *Good account of dance music & orchestra of Ganza, with notation of seven songs.*

5—WEST AFRICA

VILLAULT, *Le Sieur.* Relation des costes d'Afrique appellées Guinée. *pp.*310–18. Paris : Thierry. 1669.

„ *English ed. of above.* Relation of the coasts of Africk called Guinée. *pp.*216–23. For John Starkey. 1670.
> *Interesting observations on drums, flutes, guitar & dancing.*

ISERT, PAUL ERDMANN. Neue Reise nach Guinea. *pp.*31, 141, 191–2. Berl. 1790.
> *Xylo. & other instr. descr. in some detail.*

HOVELACQUE, ABEL. Les nègres de l'Afrique sus-equatoriale. *pp.*374–85, *et seq.* Paris : Lecrosnier. 1889.
> *Contains many references to music & instr. of W. Afr. tribes from earlier sources.*

GALERNE, MAURICE [*i.e.* G. MAURICE]. Le théatre, la danse et la musique indigènes aux colonies françaises [L'Illustré, Lyons, Nov. 1912–June 1913]
> *A popular general account.*

BALLANTA, NICHOLAS GEORGE JULIUS. An African scale [Music. Courier, 84/26 : 6 : 1922]
> *Notes on the W. African scale & cadences, illust. by notation.*

„ Gathering folk tunes in the African country [Music. America, 44/23 : 3, 11 : 1926]
> *Remarks on character of W. Afr. music, instr., intonation & melody, with notation.*

BUTT-THOMPSON, FREDERICK WILLIAM. West African secret societies. *pp.*162–67. Witherby. 1929.
> *Informative remarks on ritual instr.*

BALLANTA, NICHOLAS GEORGE JULIUS. Music of the African races [West Africa, 14 : 752–53 : 1930]

„ *Ditto : extracts.* *In* Negro Yearbook, ed. M. N. Work. *pp.*441–44. Tuskegee. 1931–32.
> *General account of W. Afr. music : with an estimate of the effects of western music on native form & rhythm.*

WILLIAMS, L. HENDERSON. European music tests applied to W. Afr. natives [Education Outlook, 19–20 : 1933]

KOHN, *** West and East African songs. *In* Negro Anthology, ed. Nancy Cunard. *pp.*416–18. Wishart. 1934.
> *Contains notation of six W. Afr. melodies.*

GORER, GEOFFREY. Africa dances. 363*pp.* Faber. 1935.
> *General account of W. Afr. dances, with no specific descr. of music or instr.*

6—FRENCH SUDAN & NIGER COLONY

PARK, MUNGO. Travels in the interior districts of Afr. *pp.*278–79. Nicol. 1799.

„ *Ditto* [Pinkerton's Voyages, 5 : 878 : 1808–14]
> *Observations on instr., handclapping & extempore songs of Mandingo, with notation of one song.*

LYON, GEORGE FRANCIS. Narrative of travels in Northern Africa, 1818, 1819, & 1820. *pp.*161, 234. Murray. 1821.
> *Brief note on singing & gourd instr. of Tibbu.*

CAILLIÉ, RENÉ. Journal d'un voyage à Temboctou et à Jenné. *v.*1, *pp.*360, 428–29 : *v.*2, *pp.*34, 72–73, 105–06. Paris : Imprimerie Royale. 1830.

„ Travels through Central Africa to Timbuctoo, 1824–28. *v.*1, *pp.*369, 391–92. Colburn. 1830.
> *Incidental descr. of dances, music & instr. of Mandingo, & Bambara peoples.*

CROZALS, J. de. Les Peulhs. *pp.*176, 239. Paris : Maisonneuve. 1883.
> *Notes on musical instr. : with quotations from earlier travellers.*

LENZ, OSKAR. Timbuktu. *v.*2, *pp.*217–18. Leip. : Brockhaus. 1884.
> *Note on professional singers.*

GALLIENI, *Le Commandant.* Voyage au Soudan-Français, 1879–81. *p.*40. Paris : Hachette. 1885.
> *Bambara orchestra descr.*

BISSUEL, H. Les Tuareg de l'Ouest. *pp.*99–100. Alger : Jourdan. 1888.
> *Descr. monochord, flutes & drums.*

BINGER, LOUIS GUSTAVE. Du Niger au Golfe de Guinée par le pays de Kong et le Mossi. *v.*1, *pp.*76–77. Paris : Hachette. 1892.
> *Mention of flute & lyre.*

TELLIER, LOUIS. Autour de Kita. *pp.*176–85. Paris : Lavauzelle. [1902]
> *Detailed notes on music & instr. of Malinké : with notation of six airs.*

BAZIN, HIPPOLYTE. Les Bambara et leur langue [Anthropos, Wien, 1 : 689 : 1906]
> *Descr. of instr. : one paragraph only.*

DELAFOSSE, MAURICE. Le peuple Siéna ou Sénoufo [Rev. Etud. Ethnog. Sociol., 4–5 : 267–69 : 1908]
> *Brief observations on songs & singing, with descr. of instr.*

JEAN, CAMILLE CHARLES. Les Touareg du Sud-Est l'Aïr. *pp.*209–14. Paris : Larose. 1909.
> *Notes on instr. & singing.*

HENRY, JOSEPH. Les Bambara. *pp.*146–47. Wien : Anthropos Bibliothek. 1910. *i.*
> *Descr. ritual trumpets & harp.*

CHÉRON, GEORGES. Les Minianka [Rev. Etud. Ethnog. Sociol., 4 : 185–86 : 1913]
> *Short note on griots & instr.*

MONTEIL, CHARLES. Les Khassonké. *pp.*132–34. Paris : Leroux. 1915.
> *Descr. professional musicians, instr. of chiefs' orchestras & dances.*

TAUXIER, LOUIS. Le noir du Yatenga. *pp.*315, 522. Paris : Larose. [1917]
> *Brief notes on characteristics of music.*

ANON. Un instr. soudanais : la kora. *In* Encyclopédie de la musique et dictionnaire du Conservatoire, ed. Lavignac, *v.*5, *pt.*1, *pp.*3224–25. Paris. 1922.

ABADIE, MAURICE. Afrique centrale : la colonie du Niger. *pp*.193–95. Paris. 1927. *i*.
> *Several instr. descr.*

REED, L. N. Notes on some Fulani tribes & customs [Africa, 5 : 436, 438 : 1932]
> *Drum & horn descr.*

LUTTEN, ERIC. Les wasamba et leur usage dans la circoncision [Minotaure, Paris, 2 : 13–17 : 1933] *i*.
> *Notes on ceremonial calabash-rattle, well illustrated.*

RAIMOND, GEORGES. De la musique chez les Bambaras aux Jazz modernes [Monde Colonial Illustré, Paris, 145 : 162 : 1935]
> *Short account of rhythm & orchestration, with notation of song, & drum & xylophone accompaniment.*

NOIROT, ERNEST. A travers le Fouta-Diallon et le Bambouc. *pp*.326–45. Paris : Dreyfous. n.d.
> *Chapter on music, instr., & dancing of Malinké, Fula & Bambara, with notation of several airs.*

7—PORTUGUESE GUINEA AND LIBERIA

CORRY, JOSEPH. Observations upon the Windward Coast of Afr. *pp*.67–68, 153–54. Nicol. 1807. *i*.
> *Notes on drums, xylos & " monotonous songs ".*

BÜTTIKOFER, J. Einiges über die Eingeborenen von Liberia [Intern. Archiv Ethnog., 1 : 87–88 : 1888] *i*.
> *Brief descr. of instr., singing & dancing : see plates* 13–15.

DÖLTER, CORNELIUS. Über die Capverden nach dem Rio Grande und Futah-Djallon. *pp*.195 *et seq*. Leip. : Frohberg. 1888.
> *Descr. instr. & dancing of Fula, Mandingo, Balanta & Papel.*

BÜTTIKOFER, J. Reisebilder aus Liberia. *v*.2, *pp*.334–48. Leiden : Brill. 1890. *i*.
> *Drums, rattles, harp & horn descr.*

LEPRINCE, M. Notes sur les Mancagnes [L'Anthrop., 16 : 65 : 1905]
> *Brief mention of flute & drum.*

JOHNSTON, *Sir* HARRY HAMILTON. Liberia. *v*.2, *p*.1026. Hutchinson. 1906. *i*.
> *Brief mention of instr. : rattles & trumpets illust.*

NÉEL, H. Note sur deux peuplades de la frontière libérienne, les Kissi et les Tomas [L'Anthrop., 24 : 465 : 1913]
> *Note on singing of griots, flute & horn orchestras.*

WESTERMANN, DIEDRICH H. Die Kpelle. 552*pp*. Göttingen : Vandenhoeck. 1921.
> *See index : Musikinstr. & Zaubermusiker.*

HEINITZ, WILHELM. Analyse eines Mendes-Liedes [Vox, Hamburg, 9 : 40–44 : 1928]
> *Contains notation from phonog. recording, & full discussion.*

SHATTUCK, GEORGE C. Liberia & the Belgian Congo [Jour. R. Geog. Soc., 46 : 229 : 1929]
> *Descr. of Mandingo water drum, signal drums & Kpelle rattle.*

STRONG, RICHARD. The African Republic of Liberia & the Belgian
Congo. *v.*1, *pp.*55, 64–66. Camb., Mass.: Harvard U.P. 1930. *i.*
> *Short account of Mandingo & Kpelle music & instr.*

BERNATZIK, HUGO ADOLF. Meine Expedition nach Portugiesisch
Guinea [Atlantis, Leip., 1 : 197–208 : 1932] *i.*
> *Includes a good illust. of Balanta drummer.*

,, Äthiopen des Westens. *v.*1, *pp.*279 *et seq.*, & plates in *v.*2. Wien :
Seidel. 1933.
> *Excellent illust. of Balanta & Fulup instr., showing manner of
> playing, with comments on these.*

GERMANN, PAUL. Die Völkerstämme in Norden von Liberia. *pp.*62–
66, 117. Leip.: Voigtländer. 1933. *i.*
> *Useful notes on Toma instr. (see Plate XX, etc.), Kru harp, &
> music & singing in mask festivals.*

BERNATZIK, HUGO ADOLF. Afrikanische Musikinstrumente [Atlantis,
Leip., 6 : 645–51 : 1934] *i.*
> *Excellent illust. of Balanta, Fulup & Mandingo instr., showing
> manner of playing & construction.*

8—SENEGAL

JOBSON, RICHARD. The golden trade : or a discovery of the river
Gambra. *pp.*105–08. Okes. 1623.

,, *Ditto.* Ed. by C. G. Kingsley [Mary Kingsley Travel Books No. 1]
*pp.*133–36. Teignmouth : Speight & Walpole. [1623] 1904.
> *Informative observations on song ceremonies & several instr.*

LEMAIRE, JACQUES JOSEPH. Les voyages du Sieur Lemaire aux isles.
Canaries, . . . Senegal et Gambie. *pp.*120–23. Paris : Collombat.
1695.
> *Entertaining notes on drums, xylo & praise-songs.*

FROGER, FRANÇOIS. Relation of a voyage made in . . . 1695. *pp.*35–
36. Gillyflower. 1698. *i.*
> *Descr. & illust. of a xylophone seen ' near Gorea '.*

LABAT, JEAN BAPTISTE. Nouvelle relation de l'Afrique occidentale.
*v.*2, *pp.*329–33. Paris : Cavelier. 1728.
> *Contains good descr. of xylo, drums, trumpets & flutes.*

DEMANET, *L'Abbé.* Nouvelle histoire de l'Afrique françoise. *v.*2,
*pp.*69–70. Paris : Duchesne. 1767.
> *Descr. a xylophone in some detail.*

LABARTHE, P. Voyage au Sénégal, 1784–85. *pp.*165–66. Paris :
L'auteur. 1802.
> *Descr. stringed instr. & drum.*

GRAY, WILLIAM G. & DOCHARD, *** Travels in Western Africa,
1818–21. *pp.*54, 301. Murray. 1825. *i.*
> *Brief descr. of Mandingo drums, lyre, xylo & flute.*

VERNEUIL, V. L'art musical au Sénégal et dans l'Afrique centrale.
Paris. 1848.
> *Title taken from Bailly (infra) : contains notation.*

BOILAT, P. D. Esquisses sénégalaises. *pp.*313–15. Paris : Bertrand. 1853.
  Account of Wolof griots & their music.
HECQUARD, HYACINTE. .Voyage sur la Côte. *p.*123. Paris : Impri-
  merie de Bénard. 1855.
  Descr. instr. of Mandingo.
RAFFENEL, ANNE. Nouveau voyage dans le pays des Nègres. *v.*1,
  *pp.*40, 430. Paris : Chaix. 1856.
  Descr. of singing & a xylophone.
BÉRENGER-FÉRAUD, L. J. B. Les peuplades de la Sénégambie.
  *pp.*95–96, 191–92, 213, 240, 327, 333, 375–76. Paris : Leroux : 1879.
  Brief notes on instr. of Soninké, Mandingo, Bambara, Fula, Nalou.
  „ Etude sur les griots des peuplades de la Sénégambie [Rev. Ethnog.,
  5 : 266–79 : 1882]
  *Informative account of professional musicians & their social
  importance.*
BAILLY, EDMOND. Le pittoresque musical à l'Exposition [L'Humanité
  Nouvelle, Paris, 177–92 : 1900]
  *General remarks on griots & instr., chiefly derivative, with notation
  of kora airs.*
LASNET, Dr. Une mission au Sénégal. *pp.*35–36, 57, 95, 135. Paris :
  Challamel. 1900. *i.*
  Brief notes on instr. of Mandingo, Wolof, & Fula tribes.
FORWERG, RUDOLPH. Die Bewohner der Guineaküste [Jahr. Verh.
  Erdk. Dres., 27 : 139–40 : 1901]
  Notes on singing, instr. & dancing.
BELLILE, *** Notes sur la musique orientale : lettres et photographies
  du Haut-Sénégal et de Batavia [Rev. Music., 5 : 564–65 : 1905] *i.*
  Brief note on a marimba, giving its interval-range.
CHÉRON, GEORGES. Les Minianka [Rev. Etud. Ethnog. Sociol., 4 :
  185–86 : 1913]
  Note on instr. & singing.
GRANNER, ERWIN. Ein afrikanisches Musikinstrument [Kosmos,
  Stuttgart, 10 : 269–70 : 1913] *i.*
  Descr. of a kora (stringed instr.)
ADAM, PAUL. La musique et le ballet au Sénégal [S.I.M., Paris, 10 :
  6–9 : 1914]
  A general account dealing chiefly with dance-ritual.
PERRON, MICHEL. Chants populaires de la Sénégambie et du Niger
  [Bul. Ag. Génl. Col., 23 : 803–11 : 1930]
  Study of the griots & their songs : incidental mention of instr.

9—FRENCH GUINEA, UPPER VOLTA & IVORY COAST

DELAFOSSE, MAURICE. Les Agnis [L'Anthrop., 4 : 439–40 : 1893]
  Notation of four tunes given : notes on choral singing.
EYSSÉRIC, M. J. Rapport sur une mission scientifique à la Côte d'Ivoire
  [Nouvelles Archives des Missions Scientifiques, Paris, ser.4, v.9 :
  248–49 : 1899]
  *Notes on Baoulé & Gouro instr. : with notation of a Baoulé air &
  xylo scale.*

DELAFOSSE, MAURICE. Sur des traces probables de civilisation égyptienne et d'hommes de race blanche à la Côte d'Ivoire [L'Anthrop., 11 : 451 : 1900]
> Short note estimating Egyptian influence on Baoulé musical instr.

RUELLE, E. Notes sur quelques populations noires de l'A.O.F. [L'Anthrop., 15 : 659, 683 : 1904]
> Brief descr. of instr. of Lobi & Mossi.

THOMANN, GEORGES. Essai de manuel de la langue néouolé. pp.27–28, 147–56, 173–74. Paris : Leroux. 1905.
> Contains list of instr. & notation of three songs.

WERNER, ALICE. Language & folklore in W. Africa [Jour. Afr. Soc., 6 : 76 : 1906]
> Contains notation of air from Thomann (supra).

MACLAUD, Dr. Note sur un instr. de musique employé au Fouta-Dialon [L'Anthrop., 19 : 271–73 : 1908] i.
> Note on a friction-drum.

BRISLEY, THOMAS. Some notes on the Baoulé tribe [Jour. Afr. Soc., 8 : 300 : 1909]
> Brief mention of a sansa.

MARC, LUCIEN. Les pays Mossi. p.127. Paris : Larose. 1909. i.
> Illustration of drums being played.

JOYEUX, CHARLES. Notes sur quelques manifestations musicales observées en Haute Guinée [Rev. Music., 10 : 49–58 : 1910 ; & 11 : 103–04 : 1911]
> Detailed descr. of Malinké instr. : remarks on singing, & ritual & dance music.

CHÉRUY, P. Notes sur les Agnis de l'Indénié [Rev. Etud. Ethnog. Sociol. : 231–32 : 1914]
> Descr. several instr.

PROUTEAUX, MAURICE. Notes sur certains rites magico-religieux de la Haute Côte d'Ivoire : les Gbons [L'Anthrop., 29 : 44–45 : 1919]
> Brief note on ritual instr.

JOYEUX, CHARLES. La musique chez les nègres de la Haute-Guinée [L'Anthrop., 33 : 549–50 : 1923]
> Synopsis only of a paper on this subject : see infra.

,, Etude sur quelques manifestations musicales observées en Haute-Guinée française [Rev. Ethnog. Trad. Pop., 5 : 170–212 : 1924] i.
> Good descr. of Malinké instr. : notes on ceremonial music & dancing.

THOMAS, JEAN. La Guinée et le Niger [La Géographie, Paris, 49 : 455, 457 : 1928]
> Contains notation of boat songs & xylo airs.

PROUTEAUX, MAURICE. Le culte de Séké [Rev. Ethnog. Trad. Pop., 7 : 173 et seq. : 1931]
> Notes on ritual drums & rattles.

LABOURET, HENRI. Un grand tambour de bois ebrié [Bul. Mus Ethnog. Troc., 2 : 48–55 : 1931] i.
> Good descr. of slit-drum : with note by A. Schaeffner.

LABOURET, HENRI. Les tribus du Rameau Lobi [Trav. Mém. Inst. Ethnol., 15 : 192–99 : 1931] *i.*

> *Good descr. of xylos, drums & harps, songs, whistle-language & dancing.*

JOURDAIN, M. Un instr. du pays Bobo (Haute Volta) [L'Anthrop., 42 : 676 : 1932]

> *Note & discussion on zither instr. See also* Montandon : Nouveaux exemplaires africains de la cithare en radeau, *in section* 10 *infra.*

HEIM, ARNOLD. Negro Sahara von der Guineaküste zum Mittelmeer. *pp.*31, 39, 64–65, 95. Bern : Huber. 1934. *i.*

> *Notes on Lobi dance & Baoulé singing & instr., with notation.*

10—TOGO

HENRICI, ERNST. Das deutsche Togogebiet und meine Afrikareise, 1887. *pp.*63–64. Leip. : Reissner. 1888.

> *Brief descr. of several Ewe instr. : notation of one song.*

KLING, HERMANN. Bericht über seine letzte, von Lome über Kpandu, Salaga und Naparri nach Bismarckburg ausgeführte Reise [Mitt. Schutz., 3 : 162 : 1890]

> *Brief enumeration of Digbemba instr.*

HEROLD, *Hauptmann.* [Letter concerning Togo drum] [Ethnol. Notizbl., 1 : 39–40 : 1895] *i.*

WEULE, KARL. Schädeltrommeln aus dem Otschigebiet [Ethnol. Notizbl., 1 : 35–37 : 1896]

> *Descr. & discussion of several drums.*

LUSCHAN, FELIX von. Beiträge zur Volkërkunde der deutschen Schutzgebiete. *pp.*47–48. Berl. : Reimer. 1897. *i.*

PLEHN, RUDOLF. Beiträge zur Völkerkunde des Togo-Gebietes. *pp.*32–39. Halle : Univ. 1898.

> *Discussion of songs : not of much importance.*

KLOSE, HEINRICH. Togo unter deutscher Flagge. *pp.*223–24, 375–77, 439–40, 449. Berl. : Reimer. 1899. *i.*

> *Notes on instr., singing & dancing of Hausa, Kpando & other tribes.*

KARSTEN, PAULA. Wer ist mein Nächster ? Negertypen aus Deutsch-westafrika. *pp.*xxxi–xxxvii. Berl. : Gose. 1903.

> *Notes on instr., singing & dancing.*

L., P. Lieder im Gë-Dialekt (Klein-Popo, Togo) [Globus, Braunsch-weig, 79 : 349 : 1901 ; & 81 : 238 : 1903]

> *Gives words & notation of several songs.*

HEILBORN, ADOLF. Die Musik der Naturvölker unserer Kolonien [Deut. Kol. Zeit., 21 : 347–48 : 1904]

> *Contains notation of Togo airs.*

KLOSE, HEINRICH. Musik, Tanz, und Spiel in Togo [Globus, Braunsch-weig, 89 : 9–13, 69–75 : 1906] *i.*

> *Ewe & Hausa drums & other instr. descr., with notes on dance orchestras.*

SPIETH, JAKOB. Die Ewe-Stämme. *p.*61*. Berl. : Reimer. 1906. *i.*
  See also index : Trommel, & good illust.
WITTE, P. A., & SCHMIDT, WILHELM. Lieder und Gesänge der Ewhe-
  Neger (Gẽdialekt) [Anthropos, Wien, 1 : 65–81, 194–209 : 1906]
    *Contains notation from phonog. recordings & good discussion of
    folksongs : notes on relation of tone, melody & rhythm : an important
    source.*
SMEND, *Oberleut.* *** von. Negermusik und Musikinstrumente der
  Togo [Globus, Braunschweig, 93 : 71–75 : 89–94 : 1908] *i.*
    Useful account of rhythm, dance music & drums : instr. well descr.
SCHÖNHARL, JOSEF. Volkskundliches aus Togo. *pp.*154–85, 195,
  et seq. Dresden : Kochs. 1909.
    *Good descr. of Ewe drum rhythms : notation of 20 songs, with
    notes on instr.*
HORNBOSTEL, ERICH M. von. Musik der Eingeborenen. *In* Deutsches
  Kolonial Lexicon, ed. Heinrich Schnee. *v.*2, *pp.*602–05. Leip. :
  Quelle. 1920. *i.*
    Contains notation of Togo air, from Witte (supra).
ANON. Les arts à Togo [Togo-Cameroun, Paris, 6 : 154–55 : 1931]
    Note on orchestra, instr. & dancing.
MONTANDON, GEORGE. Nouveaux exemplaires africains de la cithare
  en radeau [L'Anthrop., 42 : 676–78 : 1932] *i.*
    A discussion on sansas from Togo & elsewhere.
HEINITZ, WILHELM. Musikwissenschaftliche Vergleiche a. vier afri-
  kanischen Gesängen [Vox, 21 : 23–32 : 1935]
    Contains analysis and notation of several Ewe songs.

11—DAHOMEY

DALZEL, ARCHIBALD. History of Dahomey. *pp.*54, 130, 133.
  Spilsbury. 1793. *i.*
    See interesting illust. of drums & other instr.
DUNCAN, JOHN. Travels in Western Africa in 1845 & 1846. *v.*1,
  *p.*22 ; *v.*2, *pp.*115–16, 151. Bentley. 1847.
    Detailed descr. of drum, guitar & flute-band.
SKERTCHLEY, J. ALFRED. Dahomey as it is. *pp.*18–19, 135–36,
  170–72. Chapman & Hall. 1874.
    Observant notes on instr. & singing.
BOUCHE, PIERRE. Sept ans en Afrique Occidentale. *pp.*92–97.
  Paris : Plon. 1885.
    Percussion instr. & 'mandolin' descr. : note on dances.
ALBÉCA, ALEXANDRE L. d'. Voyage au pays des Eoués [Tour du
  Monde, Paris, 1 : 98–99, 104 : 1895] *i.*
    Short account of several instr. : notation of one air.
FOÀ, EDOUARD. Le Dahomey. *pp.*250–52. Paris. 1895.
    Brief observations on singing, instr. & dancing.
HAJDUKIEWICZ de POMIAN, A. Dahome, land och folk [Ymer, Stock-
  holm, 15 : 113–15 : 1895]
    On instr., dances & accompanying rhythm & melody.

GIGLIOLO, ENRICO H. La kpwen, tromba de guerra delle **Amazzoni** del Dahomii [Archiv. Antrop. Etnol., 26 : 106–10 : 1896]
BRUNET, L. & GIETHLEN, LOUIS. Dahomey et dépendances. *v.1, pp.*333–35. Paris : Challamel. 1900.
    Brief descr. of instr., games, songs & dances.
TIERSOT, JULIEN. Notes d'ethnographie musicale : la musique **au** Dahomey [Ménestrel, Paris, 4–6 : 25–26, 33–35, 41–42 : 1903]
    Secondary source, descr. instr. & singing, with notation of several airs from earlier sources.
ANON. Notes on Dahomey songs recorded by a Dahomey youth [Mus. Jour. Phil., 2 : 54 : 1911]
HUMBERT-SAVAGEOT, M. Quelques aspects de la vie et de la **musique** dahoméennes [Zeit. f. Vergleich. Musikwiss., 2 : 76–83 : 1934]
    Discusses social function of music, with notation of 8 songs from phonog. recordings.
QUÉNUM, MAXIMILIEN. Au pays des Fons : la musique [Bul. Com. Etud. A.O.F. 18 : 323–35 : 1935]
    Instr. briefly descr. ; notes on drum rhythms & songs, with notation of 9 melodies, & short critique by F. Eboué.

12—SIERRA LEONE

GRÖBEN, OTTO FRIEDRICH von der. Guinesische Reisebeschreibung. *pp.*29, 34, 41–42, 91–92. Leip. : Reinigern. 1694. *i.*
    Descr. manner of playing drums, with notes on dance-music.
MATTHEWS, JOHN. A voyage to River Sierra Leone. *pp.*104–06. White. 1791. *i.*
    Descr. drums, guitar & other instr. of Mandingo & " Timmaneys".
WINTERBOTTOM, THOMAS MASTERMAN. Account of the native Africans in the neighbourhood of Sierra Leone. *v.1, pp.*108–14. Hatchard. 1803.
    An account in some detail of musicians, songs, drums & dances of " Timmannees " & " Foolas ".
LAING, ALEXANDER GORDON. Travels in Timannee, Kooranko & Sooliman countries in W. Afr. *pp.*368–69. Murray. 1825. *i.*
    Brief note on kora, xylo, drums & flute of the Soolima.
CLARKE, ROBERT. Sierra Leone. *pp.*57–58, 150. Ridgway. [1843]
    Notes on Tapuah dance-instr. & flutes.
GODEL, *** Ethnographie des Soussous [Bul. Soc. Anthrop. Paris, 4 : 166–67 : 1892]
    Brief account of singing, instr. & griots.
NEWLAND, HARRY OSMAN. Sierra Leone : its people, products, & secret societies. *pp.*83, 102–06. Bale. 1916.
    Descr. boat- and hammock-dances and a balangi (stringed instr.).
MARGAI, M. A. S. Music in the Protectorate of Sierra Leone [Wasu., 2 : 38–40 : 1926]
    A very general account, descr. various instr.

13—GOLD COAST AND ASHANTI.

BOSMAN, WILLEM. Nauwkeurige beschryving van de Guinese-, Goud-, en Slave-Kust. *pp.*131–33, 242. Utrecht : Schouten. 1704.

„ A new & accurate description of the Coast of Guinea. *pp.*138–40, 453. Knapton. 1705.

„ *Ditto* [Pinkerton's Voyages, 16 : 394–95, 530 : 1808–14]
Brief descr. of horn, drum & harp.

LABAT, JEAN BAPTISTE. Voyage du Chevalier des Marchais en Guinée, isles voisines, et à Cayenne, fait en 1725, 1726, & 1727. *v.*1, *p.*349 ; *v.*2, *pp.*62, 194–96, 246–50, 317. Paris : Osmont. 1730.
Descr. of ceremonial trumpets, drums & flutes seen in ' the kingdom of Juda '.

BARBOT, JOHN. A description of the coasts of North & South Guinea [Churchill's Voyages, 5/3 : 52, 55, 261, 264–65, 275, 308, 372 : 1732] *i.*
Somewhat naive descr. of drums, horns, flutes & other instr., with notes on griots & dancing.

SMITH, WILLIAM. A new voyage to Guinea. *p.*21. Nowell. 1745. *i.*
Xylophone descr. & illust.

MARRÉE, J. A. de. Reizen op en Beschrijving van de Goudkust van Guinea. *v.*2, *pp.*185–93. 'sGravenhage : Van Cleef. 1818. *i.*
Brief notes on several instr.

BOWDICH, THOMAS EDWARD. Mission from Cape Coast Castle to Ashantee. *pp.*361–69, 449–52. Murray. 1819.
Good observations on instr. & intonation : notation of several airs, harmonised.

DUPUIS, JOSEPH. Journal of residence in Ashantee. *pp.*70–71. Colburn. 1824.
Enumerates several instr., with note on choruses.

BOWDICH, THOMAS EDWARD. Excursions in Madeira & Porto Santo, 1823. *p.*210. Whittaker. 1825.
General remarks on music & air of Mandingo canoe song : of interest but no great value.

BEECHAM, JOHN. Ashantee & the Gold Coast. *pp.*167–69. Mason. 1841.
Note on flute-conversations & instr.

CRUICKSHANK, BRODIE. Eighteen years on the Gold Coast of Africa. *v.*2, *pp.*265–69. Hurst. 1853.
Remarks on form of songs, instr. & flute-ensembles.

MÄHLY, E. Zur Geographie und Ethnographie der Goldküste [Verh. f. Naturf. Gesell. in Basel, 7/3 ; 851–52 : 1885]
Informative notes on drums, horns, flute-ensembles & guitar.

ELLIS, ALFRED BURDON. The Tshi-speaking peoples of the Gold Coast of West Africa. *pp.*325–30. Chapman & Hall. 1887.
Notes on instr. & singing, with notation of several tunes.

MOLONEY, *Sir* [CORNELIUS] ALFRED. On the melodies of Ewe people of West Africa [Jour. Manch. Geog. Soc., 5 : 277–98 : 1889] *i.*
Useful account of singing & drumming, with notes on songs, & notation of several airs.

FREEMAN, RICHARD AUSTIN. Travels & life in Ashanti & Jaman. *pp*.59, 97–99, 104, 152, 257–61, 281–82, 335. Constable. 1898. *i*.
  Notes on drums, xylophone & horns, with notation of dance theme & song.

PERREGAUX, EDMOND. Chez les Achanti [Soc. Neuchât. Géog., 17 : 182–85, 235–41, 282 : 1906]
  Notes on Tshi drums, singing, dancing & instr., with notation of several airs.

VORTISCH, H. Die Neger der Goldküste [Globus, Braunschweig, 89 : 294–97 : 1906] *i*.
  Contains notation of four songs, notes on instr., singing & drumming.

ffOULKES, ARTHUR. The Company system in Cape Coast Castle [Jour. Afr. Soc., 7 : 267, 272 : 1908]
  Brief notes on drums & other ceremonial instr.

ZELLER, RUDOLF. Die Goldgewichte von Asante [Baessler Archiv, Leip., 3 : 60, 62–63 : 1912] *i*.
  Incidental mention of drums & other instr.

FISCH, RUDOLF. Die Dagbamba [Baessler Archiv, Leip., 3 : 152–53 : 1913]
  Description of drums accompanying dances.

PFISTER, G. A. Les chansons historiques et le " Timpam " des Achantis [Rev. Music., 4 : 230–35 : 1923]
  Informative notes on the songs of professional musicians & on Ashanti drums.

RATTRAY, ROBERT SUTHERLAND. Ashanti. 348*pp*. Oxf. : Clarendon Press. 1923. *i*.
  See index : Drums, Gongs, Horn-blowers : many references to ceremonial function of music.

PFISTER, G. A. Ashanti music at Empire Exhibition [Music. News, 66 : 490 : 1924]
  A brief general account.

  ,, La musica ascianti [Riv. Music. Ital., Torino, 32 : 213–18 : 1925].
  Notes on singing, drums & drum-language.

REED, E. M. G. Music of West Africa : 1—Ashanti [Music & Youth, 5 : 135–39 : 1925] *i*.
  Collection of data concerning instr. & songs, with notation of several airs including an " Ashanti traditional melody ".

WARD, WILLIAM ERNEST FRANK. Music in the Gold Coast [G.C. Rev., 3 : 199–223 : 1927]
  An important article, discussing form, intonation & rhythm of music & songs : notation of 20 airs given.

AZŬ, ENOCH. Adangbe historical & proverbial songs. 136*pp*. Accra : Govt. Printing Office. 1929.
  Includes notation of solo, chorus & drum rhythms, transcribed by W. E. F. Ward.

AMU, E. Twenty-five African songs in the Twi language. Sheldon Press. 1932.
  Music & words by the composer.

WARD, WILLIAM ERNEST FRANK. Music of the Gold Coast [Music. Times, 73 : 707–10, 797–99, 901–02 : 1932]
A comprehensive survey of native forms & traditions in music.
„ Gold Coast music in education [Oversea Educ., 5 : 64–71 : 1934]
Important discussion of the methods to be used in preserving & developing native music, especially at Achimota.

14—NIGERIA

LANDER, RICHARD LEMON. Records of Captain Clapperton's last expedition to Africa. *v.*1, *pp.*289–98. Colburn. 1830.
Observant notes on songs & instr.

D'AVEZAC, M. Notice sur le pays et le peuple des Yébous en Afrique. *pp.*86–94. Paris : Dondey-Dupré. 1845.
Gives vernacular names of instr., notes on songs & notation of several airs.

KÖLER, HERMANN. Einige notizen über Bonny an der Küste von Guinea. *pp.*35, 72, 130–31. Göttingen : Dieterichschen Univ. Buchdruckerei. 1848.
Brief descr. of ritual instr., with notation of a boat song.

NACHTIGAL, GUSTAV. Saharâ und Südân. *v.*1, *pp.*745–46 : *v.*3, *pp.*226, 437. Leip. : Brockhaus. 1889.
Instr. of Bornu orchestra descr. : mention of drum-festivals.

MURDOCH, JOHN. The whizzing stick or " Bull-Roarer " on the W. coast of Africa [Amer. Anthrop., 3 : 258 (note) : 1890]
Short appendix to Moloney's article (supra, sect. 13).

DAY, C. R. Native musical instr. *In* FERRYMAN, A. F. M. : Up the Niger. *pp.*264–81. Philip. 1892.
Good account of instr. & notes on music, with notation of several airs.

ROTH, HENRY LING. Great Benin : its customs, arts, & horrors. *pp.*77, 153–54, & index. Halifax : King. 1903. *i.*
Descr. drums & other instr., incorporating data from earlier travellers : see especially figures 151–53.

PARTRIDGE, CHARLES. Cross river natives. *pp.*226–29. Hutchinson. 1905. *i.*
Gongs, horns, xylo & drums descr. & illust.

ANON. Sur les bords du Niger [Rev. Music., 6 : 528–30 : 1906]
General remarks on types of music, and instr. & songs in myth & legend.

VISCHER, HANNS. Journeys in Northern Nigeria [Geog. Jour., 28 : 373 : 1906]
Brief descr. of a native band.

SCHULTZE, ARNOLD. Das Sultanat Bornu. *p.*95. Essen : Baedeker. 1910.
Brief note on wind instr.

TALBOT, PERCY AMAURY. In the shadow of the Bush. *pp.*297–303. Heinemann. 1912.
Notes on several Ekoi instr.

TREMEARNE, ARTHUR JOHN NEWMAN. Notes on the Kagoro & other Nigerian head-hunters [R. Anthrop. Inst., 42 : 181–82 : 1912] *i.*
Descr. horns, harp & other instr., with notation of marriage song & horn melody.

„ The tailed head-hunters of Nigeria. *pp.*249–52, 262–69. Seeley, Service. 1912.
Note on Kagoro flutes : with notation of Kagoro song & Kajji orchestral music.

ANON. Spielleute und Märchenerzähler Innerafrikas [Westermanns Monatshefte, Braunschweig, 115 : 573–85 : 1913] *i.*
Illust. of Ilorin, Hausa & Samberna instr. & players, with commentary.

THOMAS, NORTHCOTE WHITRIDGE. Anthropological report on the Ibo speaking peoples of Nigeria. *pt.*1, *p.*136. Harrison. 1913.
Short descr. of drums, rattle, flute, musical bow & sansa.

RUMANN, W. B. Funeral ceremonies for the late ex-Oba of Benin [Jour. Afr. Soc., 14 : 37–38 : 1914]
Mention of ritual drums, flutes & calabashes.

TREMEARNE, ARTHUR JOHN NEWMAN. The ban of the Bori. *pp.*251–52, 281–85. Heath. [1914]
Descr. & notation of songs of demon-dancers.

B., A. M. The ordeal of manhood [Jour. Afr. Soc., 15 : 250, *et seq.* : 1916]
Ga-Anda reed instr. & their ritual significance descr.

LUSCHAN, FELIX von. Die Altertümer von Benin [Veröff. Mus. Völk., Bd. 8–10] *pp.*175–95. Berl. 1919. *i.*
Descr. & illust. of instr. from Benin carvings : see especially plates 36–39, 41, figs. 296–319.

THOMAS, NORTHCOTE WHITRIDGE. Notes on Edo burial customs [R. Anthrop. Inst., 50 : 410–11 : 1920]
Note on form & harmony of burial songs.

BASDEN, GEORGE THOMAS. Among the Ibos of Nigeria. *pp.*185–93. Seeley, Service. 1921.
Pottery whistle & other instr. described.

FUNKE, E. Einige Tanz- und Liebeslieder der Haussa [Zeit. f. Eingeborenensprachen, 11 : 259–78 : 1921]
Incidental references in text to drums & drumming.

JOHNSON, SAMUEL. The history of the Yorubas. *pp.*120–21. Routledge. 1921.
Brief mention of drums & trumpets.

MEEK, CHARLES KINGSLEY. The Northern tribes of Nigeria. *v.*2, *pp.*155–59. Milford. 1925.
Good notes on instr. & their distribution.

REED, E. M. G.   The Nigerian at home [Music & Youth, 5 : 159–63 : 1925]   *i.*
> *Popular account of dances, songs & instr., from Day (supra), & other sources.*

PATTERSON, JOHN ROBERT.   Kanuri songs.   30*pp.*   Lagos : Government Printer.   1926.
> *Text of songs, & singing descr. : no notation.*

TALBOT, PERCY AMAURY.   Peoples of Southern Nigeria.   *v.3, pp.*807–16, 819.   Milford.   1926.   *i.*
> *Useful & accurate descr. of many instr., showing distribution among Yoruba, Edo, Ibo & Ekoi peoples : good illustrations.*

HALL, HENRY USHER.   A drum from Benin [Mus. Jour. Phil., 19 : 130–43 : 1928]   *i.*
> *Descr. in detail & compared with similar drums.*

MANSFELD, ALFRED.   Westafrika.   *pp.*45–47.   München : Müller.   1928.
> *General remarks on instr. & dancing of Ekoi.*

MEEK, CHARLES KINGSLEY.   The Katab & their neighbours [Jour. Afr. Soc., 27 : 375 : 1928]
> *Brief note on instr.*

DANIEL, F.   Note on a gong of bronze from Katsina, Nigeria [Man, 29 : 157–58 : 1929]   *i.*

MEEK, CHARLES KINGSLEY.   A Sudanese kingdom.   *pp.*458 *et seq.*   Kegan Paul.   1931.   *i.*
> *Good descr. of music & instr. of Jukuns.*

„   Tribal studies in Northern Nigeria.   *v.*1, *pp.*38, 143, 268, 290, 348, 434, 437, 461 ; *v.*2, *pp.*57–58, 301.   Kegan Paul.   1931.   *i.*
> *Good specific descr. & illust. of instr. in their social context.*

HARRIS, PERCY GRAHAM.   Notes on drums & musical instr. seen in Sokoto province, Nigeria [R. Anthrop. Inst., 62 : 105–25 : 1932]   *i.*
> *Accurate account of instr., how constructed & played.*

TALBOT, PERCY AMAURY.   Tribes of the Niger Delta.   *pp.*318–19.   Sheldon Press.   1932.   *i.*
> *Describes Ibo instr.. : illust. of drums & xylos.*

ABRAHAM, R. C.   The Tiv people.   *pp.*223–24.   Lagos : Govt. Printer.   1933.   *i.*
> *Notes on several instr. & on songs : see also pp.*107 *(note),* 130 *(note), & plates* 46, 48–49.

BAUMANN, MARGARET.   Sons of sticks : sketches of everyday life in a Nigerian bush village.   With music of Yoruba songs & marches.   *Appendix,* 12*pp.*   Sheldon Press.   1933.
> *Contains harmonised notation.*

HAMBLY, WILFRID DYSON.   Culture areas of Nigeria [Field Mus. Nat. Hist., Anthrop. Ser., *v.* 21, *No.*3]   *pp.*430–32, 462, 476.   Chicago.   1935.   *i.*
> *Descr. Fulani, Yoruba & Hausa instr. : see plates* 97, 129, 130.

BOULTON, LAURA C.   Bronze artists of W. Africa [Nat. Hist., N.Y., 36 : 17–22 : 1935]   *i.*
> *Good illust. of Benin & Ife drums & gourd-rattles.*

ALLEN, WILLIAM & THOMSON, THOMAS RICHARD HAYWOOD. A narrative of the expedition to the River Niger in 1841. *pp.*298–99. Bentley. 1848.
Descr. flutes, harp & musical bow of Bimbia, with notation of one air.

SCHWARZ, BERNHARD. Kamerun. *pp.*159–61. Leip. : Frohberg. 1886.
Describes Batwiri singing & percussion instr., with notation of two airs.

MÜLLER, ROBERT. Leben und Treiben in Kamerun [Ausland, Stuttgart, 62 : 83–84 : 1889]
Brief notes on dance instr. & boat songs.

MORGEN, CARL. Durch Kamerun von Sud nach Nord. *p.*197. Leip. : Brockhaus. 1893. *i.*
*Note on orchestra of horns & drums of Yaunde. See illust. on pp.*40, 55, 200, 278.

PASSARGE, SIEGFRIED. Adamaua. *pp.*68, 104–05, 281, 476. Berl. : Reimer. 1895. *i.*
Brief descr. of dances & instr. of Hausa, Garua, Fulbe & Mbum.

ZENKER, G. [On Yaunde music] [Mitt. Schutz., 8 : 59 : 1895]
Instr. descr. in some detail.

HÖSEMANN, *Dr.* Ethnographische Tagebuchnotizen von der Expedition gegen die Esūm, 1901 [Ethnol. Notizbl., 3 : 108–09, 111 : 1901]
Mbum drums & trumpets briefly described.

SEIDEL, AUGUST. Das Bakwirivolk in Kamerun [Beitr. Kol. Polit., 3 : 163, 170–71 : 1902]
Short notes on singing, dance, music & instr. : notation of one melody.

HUTTER, FRANZ. Wanderungen und Forschungen im Nord-Hinterland von Kamerun. *pp.*297–98, 387–88, 404 *et seq.*, 433–35. Braunschweig : Vieweg. 1902.
Notes on singing & dancing of Banyang & Bali.

„ Explorations dans l'hinterland septentrional de la colonie du Cameroun [Bul. Soc. Anthrop. Paris, 5 : 524 : 1903]
Note on singing & instr. of the Bali.

SEIDEL, AUGUST. Deutsch-Kamerun. *pp.*227–28. Berl. : Meidinger. 1906.
Descr. instr. of Bali, Duala & Hausa.

MANSFELD, ALFRED. Urwald-dokumente : vier Jahre unter den Crossflussnegern Kameruns. *pp.*133–45, & *appendix* 6. Berl. : Reimer. 1908. *i.*
Important descr. & illust. of many instr. : notes on dance music, with notation of three airs, from phonog. records.

MEYER, HANS, *ed.* Das deutsche Kolonialreich. *v.*1, *pp.*490–91. Leip. : Bibliographisches Institut. 1909. *i.*
Notes on distribution of instr. in Cameroons, with map.

ANKERMANN, BERNHARD. Ethnographische Forschungsreise ins Grasland von Kamerun [Zeit. f. Ethnol., 17 : 309 : 1910]   *i.*
Brief descr. of Bali xylophone.

BUFE, *** Die Bakundu [Archiv f. Anthrop., 40 : 229–30 : 1913]
Short note on instr., dance & song.

„ Die Poesie der Duala-Neger in Kamerun [Archiv f. Anthrop., 40 : 60 : 1915]
Note on songs, with notation of two boat songs.

THORBECKE, FRANZ & THORBECKE, MARIE PAULINE. Im Hochland von Mittel-Kamerun, Pt.3 [Abh. Hamburger Kol. Inst., 41] *pp.*107–17. 1919.   *i.*
Good notes on music, songs & singing.

HEINITZ, WILHELM. Musikinstrumente und Phonogramme des Ost-Mbamlandes. *In* THORBECKE : Im Hochland von Mittel-Kamerun, pt.3. *pp.*121–78, & append. [20*pp.*] [Abh. Hamburger Kol. Inst., 41] 1919.   *i.*
Detailed descr. of instr. of Tikar, Wute, Mbum & Bali : analysis of many airs with notation from phonog. recordings.

MALCOLM, L. W. G. Notes on the religious beliefs of the Eghāp, Central Cameroon [Folk Lore, 33 : 360 : 1922]
Short note on ritual instr. & flute ensemble.

DÜHRING, F. K. Die Bevölkerung des Logone Bezirks [Mitt. Schutz, 33 : 69 : 1925]
Note on instr. of Lakka.

REIN-WUHRMANN, ANNA. Mein Bamumvolk im Grasland von Kamerun. *pp.*63–66. Stuttgart : Evang. Missions-Verlag. 1925.
Somewhat vague remarks on drum-festival, with notation of a dance-tune.

SIEBER, J. Die Wute. *pp.*96–99. Berl. : Reimer. 1925.   *i.*
Notes on several instr., singing & improvisation.

TESSMANN, GÜNTER. Die Mbaka-Limba, Mbum & Lakka [Zeit. f. Ethnol., 60 : 315, 328–29, 344 : 1928]
Brief account of instr. of these tribes.

NICOL, YVES. La tribu des Bakoko. *pp.*196–99. Paris : Larose. 1929.
Enumeration of instr., notes on dancing & singing.

SCHAEFFNER, ANDRÉ. Notes sur la musique des populations du Cameroun septentrional [Minotaure, Paris, 2 : 65–70 : 1933]   *i.*
Full account of instr., rhythm, melody & songs of Fulbe & Kirdi : good illust.

SALASC, LÉON. Sur les musiques du Haut Cameroun [Togo-Cameroun, Paris, 34–45 : Jan. 1934]   *i.*
Discussion on the melodies, rhythms & dances of the Falli, Moundan & Schoas, with notation of dance motif.

TESSMANN, GÜNTER. Die Bafia. *pp.*161, 169–76. Stuttgart : Strecker. 1934.   *i.*
Good detailed descr. of instr., how constructed & played : with many illust. (See plates 21–24)

16—GABON AND MIDDLE CONGO

Du Chaillu, Paul Belloni. Explorations & adventures in Equatorial Africa. *pp.*80–81, 87–88, 201, 391. Murray. 1861. *i.*

„ Voyages et aventures dans l'Afrique equatoriale. *pp.*156–57, 164, 440. Paris : Lévy. 1863. *i.*

  Occasional notes on Fang & Bakalai instr.

Burton, *Sir* Richard Francis. A day among the Fans [Trans. Ethnol. Soc., 3 : 44 : 1865]

  Brief descr. of drum & ' harmonicon ' accompanying dance.

Lenz, Oskar. Skizzen aus Westafrika. *pp.*88, 110–11, 286–87, 301. Berl. : Hofmann. 1878.

  Brief note on Fang & other instr.

Güssfeldt, Paul, Falkenstein, J., & Pechuel-Loesche, E. Die Loango-Expedition, 1873–76. *v.*1, *pp.*76, 128–29 : *v.*2, *pp.*97, 111–32, 260. Leip. : Frohberg. 1879–82. *i.*

  Notes on Bakunya drum : good descr. of Bafiote instr. & songs, with notation of flute air & several songs.

Hübbe-Schleiden, K. Ethiopien : studien über Westafrika. *pp.*138–40, 172, 201–03. Hamburg : Friederichsen. 1879.

  Descr. music of Fang & Kru, with attempted notation of two airs.

Johnston, *Sir* Harry Hamilton. The river Congo. *pp.*432–34. Sampson Low. 1884.

  Notes on Bateke drum, horns & lyre, & on pentatonic scale.

Barret, Paul. L'Afrique occidentale. *v.*2, *pp.*227–28. Paris : Challamel. 1888.

  Briefly descr. instr. of Fang.

Guiral, Léon. Le Congo Français. *pp.*174–75. Paris : Plon. 1889.

  Brief account of instr. & singing of Bateke.

Tiersot, Julien. Musiques pittoresques. *pp.*99–108. Paris : Fischbacher. 1889.

  Secondary source, assembling data on Fang instr. & music, with notation of several airs.

Largeau, Victor. Encyclopédie pahouine. *pp.*163–65, 470. Paris : Leroux. 1901.

  See Chants, Musique : list of instr. given.

Desvallons, Gilbert. La musique et la danse au Gabon [Rev. Music., 3 : 215–18 : 1903]

  Notes on dancing, and notation of a " marinja " air & dance melodies.

Roche, Jean Baptiste. Au pays des Pahouins. *p.*92. Paris : Lavauzelle. 1904.

  Brief descr. of slit drum & stringed instr.

Avelot, R. La musique chez les Pahouins, les Bakalai, Eshira, Iveia, Bavili [L'Anthrop., 16 : 287–93 : 1905] *i.*

  Account of several instr., with notation of an Iveia melody.

Trilles, Henri. La marimba et l'anzang [Rev. Music., 5 : 473–74 : 1905] *i.*

  Descr. construction, range & performance of a Gabon marimba : note on Fang scale & seven-stringed harp.

49

BRUEL, GEORGES. Les Pomo et les Boumali [Rev. Ethnog., 1 : 27 : 1910]
>   *Brief descr. of drums, horns & bells.*

GAND, FERNAND. Les Mandja [Coll. Mon. Ethnog. No. 8] pp.239–40, 363–74. Bruxelles. 1911.
>   *Notes on dances & songs : descr. manufacture & mode of playing of drums.*

REGNAULT, M. Les Babenga [L'Anthrop., 22 : 280 : 1911]
>   *Short account of dance instr.*

MILLIGAN, ROBERT H. The fetish folk of West Africa. pp.72–84. N.Y. : Revell. 1912.
>   *Characteristics of W. Afr. music discussed : gives notation of dance & canoe songs of Gabon.*

TRILLES, HENRI. Chez les Fang. pp.87–91, 180. Lille : Soc. St. Augustin. 1912.
>   *Gives notation of several melodies.*

„ Le totémisme chez les Fan. pp.88–92, 267–79, 333–34, 373–83, 513–14, 533–36, 620. Wien : Anthropos–Bibliothek. 1912.
>   *Notes on dances & songs, with notation of ritual melodies.*

HORNBOSTEL, ERICH M. von. *In* TESSMANN, GÜNTER : Die Pangwe. v.2, pp.320–57. Berl. : Wasmuth. 1913. *i.*
>   *Important discussion of general characteristics of Fang music : good descr. of instr., with analysis & annotation of fifteen melodies in notation from phonog. recordings.*

LARSONNEUR, A. Notes sur les Pongoués [Rev. Anthrop., 24 : 189 : 1914]
>   *Short account of instr. & singing.*

BRUEL, GEORGES. L'Afrique Equatoriale Française. pp.183–85. Paris : Larose. 1918.
>   *Brief notes on instr., distribution & singing of Bateke & Banziri.*

DARRÉ, E. Notes sur la tribu des Bomitaba [Rev. Ethnog. Trad. Pop., 12 : 324 : 1922]
>   *Occasional notes on dances, orchestra & river songs.*

GRÉBERT, FERNAND. Au Gabon. pp.89–96. Paris : Soc. Miss. Evang. 1922. *i.*
>   *Observations on nature of singing, & on drums & other instr.*

„ L'art musical chez les Fang [Archiv. Suisses Anthrop. Générale, 5 : 75–86 : 1928–29] *i.*
>   *Many instr. well descr. & illust.*

LE ROY, ALEXANDRE. Les Pygmées : négrilles d'Afrique et négritos d'Asie. pp.129–30. Paris : Beauchesne. 1928. *i.*
>   *Note on Fang horn.*

MAIGNAN, *** Etudes sur le pays Pahouins [Bul. Soc. Rech. Cong., 90 : 1930]
>   *Brief mention of dances & instr.*

CHAUVET, STÉPHEN. Musique et arts nègres en A. E. F. [Sud-Ouest Economique, Bordeaux, 11 : 987–91 : 1930] *i.*

„ *Ditto* [Apollon, Paris, July 1931] [39pp.]
>   *Summary of data from Trilles & other writers : notes on instr., notation of several airs.*

17—FERNANDO PO AND RIO MUNI

IRADIER, MANUEL. Africa, viajes y trabajos de la associacion Euskara. *v.2, pp.*269–81. Vitoria : La Exploradora. 1887.
> *Good account of songs, dances & instr. of Rio Muni by D. Uruñuela, with notation of melodies, ' harmonised '.*

BAUMANN, OSCAR. Eine africanische Tropen-Insel. *pp.*98–100. Wien : Hölzel. 1888.
> *Account of clarinet, drums, ' jewsharp ' & percussion instr. of the Bubi.*

KINGSLEY, MARY. Travels in West Africa. *pp.*66–67. Macmillan. 1897.
> *Brief descr. of Bubi bow, fifes, rattles & drums.*

JOHNSTON, *Sir* HARRY HAMILTON. George Grenfell & the Congo. *v.2, p.*959. Hutchinson. 1908.
> *Note on Bubi gongs, flutes, whistle & musical bow.*

TESSMANN, GÜNTER. Die Bubi auf Fernando Po. *p.*218. Hagen : Folkwang. 1923.
> *Mention of instr.*

18—BELGIAN CONGO

ANGELO, MICHAEL &·CARLI de PIACENZA, DENIS. Voyage to Congo, 1666–7 [Pinkerton's Voyages, 16 : 160 : 1814]
„ *Ditto* [Churchill's Voyages, 1 : 563–64 : 1723]
> *Descr. of marimba, drums & iron bells.*

CARLI de PIACENZA, DENIS. Der nach Venedig überbrachte Mohr. *pp.*40–41. Augsburg. 1692.
> *Observant descr. of Bamba instr.*

PROYART, L. BONAVENTURE. Histoire de Loango. *pp.*112–15. Paris : Berton. 1766.
> *Descr. of instr., dancing & songs.*

POGGE, PAUL. Im Reiche des Muata Jamvo. *p.*241. Berl. : Reimer. 1880.
> *Brief account of Mussumba instr.*

CAMERON, VERNEY LOVETT. Across Africa. *pp.*186, 250, 267, 355. Philip. 1885. *i.*
> *Brief account of gourd rattles, kinanda, marimba & Basonge band.*

BAUMANN,. OSCAR. Beiträge zur Ethnographie des Congo [Mitt. Anthrop. Gesell. Wien, 17 : 166–79 : 1887]
„ *Ditto : separately.* 22*pp.* Wien. 1887.
> *Notes on singing & instr. of the Bakongo, Bateke, Bayanzi, Bangala & Marundscha.*

BENTLEY, W. HOLMAN. Dictionary & grammar of Kongo language. *pp.*142 *et seq.* Baptist Miss. Soc. 1887.
> *See :* Musical instr.

CHAVANNE, JOSEF. Reisen und Forschungen im alten und neuen Kongostaate. *pp.*401–02. Jena : Costenoble. 1887.
> *Notes on rhythm, drums & songs of Bafiote.*

MÖLLER, P., PAGELS, G. T. & GLEERUP, E. Tre år i Kongo. v.1,
    pp.98, 135, 167, 274 : v.2, p.147. Stockholm : Norstedt. 1887. i.
    Brief descr. of Bakongo & other instr.
COQUILHAT, CAMILLE. Sur le Haut-Congo. p.364. Paris : Lebègue.
    1888. i.
    Short account of Bangala instr.
FRANÇOIS, CURT von. Die Erforschung des Tschuapa und Lulongo.
    pp.101, 138, 173. Leip. : Brockhaus. 1888. i.
    Ivory horns, drums, sansa & bell descr.
WISSMANN, HERMANN, & WOLF, LUDWIG. Im innern Afrikas. pp.253–
    54. Leip. : Brockhaus. 1888.
    Brief mention of Bakuba instr.
ANON. [On Congo music] [Congo Illustré, Brux., 27 : 216 : 1892]
    Notation of three airs (from Wissmann, Reichard & Schweinfurth).
 ,, Les tambours [Congo Illustré, Brux., 19 : 152 : 1893] i.
    *Notes on drums from the collection of the Compagnie Belge du
    Congo.*
WILVERTH, Lieut. Chez les Mongwandies [Congo Illustré, Brux., 22 :
    175 : 1894]
    Mention of a dance orchestra.
ANON. La musique [à Congo] [Belg. Col., 1 : 565–68 : 1895–96]
    Brief account of Bangala instr., with notation of several melodies.
TORDAY, EMIL. On the trail of the Bushongo. p.46. Seeley Service.
    1895.
    Note on songs & instr. of Baluba.
VEREYECKEN, *** La région des cataractes [Congo Illustré, Brux.,
    19 : 148 : 1895] i.
    Brief account of several (Azande ?) instr.
NYS, F. Chez les Abarambos. pp.90–91, 126–28. Anvers : Huy-
    brechts. 1896.
    Scattered references to wind instr., guitar, drums & songs.
DENNETT, RICHARD EDWARD. Notes on the folk-lore of the Fjort
    [Folk-Lore Society] pp.150–63. 1898.
    Notation & discussion of several songs.
NYS, F. Le chant, les danses, la musique [Belg. Col., 3 : 509–12 : 1898]
    *General remarks on songs, dancing & instr., with notation of
    several airs (one ' arranged for piano ').*
TILKENS, E. Les Ababua [Belg. Col., 5 : 254 : 1900]
    Mention of instr.
ANON. Ethnographie congolaise : musique, chant et danse [Belg. Col.,
    7 : 557–58, et seq. : 1902 ; & 8 : 5–7, et seq. : 1903]
    *Summary of data from Wissmann, Schweinfurth, etc., with
    notation.*
MUSÉE DU CONGO, Tervueren. Notes analytiques sur les collections
    ethnographiques [Ann. Mus. Congo Belge, Ser. III : Ethnog.]
    v.1, pp.5–144. 1902–06. i. 21 plates.
    *Important account of Congo music, profusely illustr., showing
    manner of constructing & playing instr., & their social
    significance.*

SCHMELTZ, JOHANNES DIEDRICH EDUARD. Ethnographisch Album van het Stroomgebied van den Congo [Publicatien van's Rijks Ethnographisch Museum, Serie 2, No. 2] 'sGravenhage. Plates 183–98. 1904–16.
> *Good illust. of many instr.*

TORDAY, EMIL. Songs of the Baluba of Lake Moero [Man, 4 : 117–19 : 1904] *i.*
> *Useful notes on singing : notation of four melodies.*

VÉDY, Dr. Les A-Babuas [Soc. R. Belge Géog., 28 : 275–76 : 1904]
> *General remarks on songs, singers & instr.*

CALLEWAERT, E. Les Mousserongos [Soc. R. Belge Géog., 29 : 200 : 1905]
> *Note on xylo & drum.*

HARRISON, JAMES J. Life among the pygmies. *p.*18. Hutchinson. 1905. *i.*
> *Brief descr. of drums, cane-rattles & clappers accompanying dance.*

TORDAY, EMIL & JOYCE, THOMAS ATHOL. Notes on the ethnography of the Ba-Mbala [R. Anthrop. Inst., 35 : 413–14 : 1905]
> *Notes on singing & instr. : notation of two songs given.*

WINTERSGILL, H. G. Orchestras of central Africa [S. Workman, 34 : 657–62 : 1905] *i.*
> *Popular account of Congo orchestras.*

TORDAY, EMIL & JOYCE, THOMAS ATHOL. Notes on the ethnography of the Ba-Yaka [R. Anthrop. Inst., 36 : 47 : 1906]
> *Short note on friction-drum & singing.*

„ Notes on the ethnography of the Ba-Huana [R. Anthrop. Inst., 36 : 287 : 1906]
> *Mention of instr.*

VÉDY, Dr. Ethnographie congolaise : les riverains de l'Uellé [Soc. R. Belge Géog., 30 : 311–15 : 1906]
> *Gives notation of two Bakongo songs : account of dances & instr.*

HAMMAR, J. Babwende. *In* NORDENSKIÖLD, ERLAND. Etnografiska bidrag af Svenska Missionärer i Afrika. *pp.* 151–52. Stockholm : Palmquist. 1907.
> *Notation of two melodies : detailed notes on instr.*

HARROY, F. Ethnographie congolaise : les Bakubas [Soc. R. Belge Géog., 31 : 237–46 : 1907] *i.*
> *Descr. of dance & accompanying orchestra, with notation of two airs.*

OVERBERGH, CYRILLE van. Les Bangala [Coll. Mon. Ethnog., No.1] *pp.*305–14. Brux. 1907.
> *Notation of three river songs, with notes on instr.*

„ Les Mayombe [Coll. Mon. Ethnog. No. 2] *pp.*333–37. Brux. 1907.
> *Notes on singing & instr.*

TORDAY, EMIL & JOYCE, THOMAS ATHOL. On the ethnology of the South-West Congo Free State [R. Anthrop. Inst., 37 : 150 : 1907]
> *Descr. marimbas of the Ba-Kwese.*

DELHAISE, CHARLES. Chez les Warembas [Soc. R. Belge Géog., 32 : 263–67 : 1908]   *i.*
> *Notes on instr. of men & women, & on singing & songs, with notation of several melodies.*

,, Chez les Warundi et les Wahorohoro [Soc. R. Belge Géog., 32 : 413–14 : 1908]
> *Several instr. desr. : brief note on character of music.*

JOHNSTON, *Sir* HARRY HAMILTON. George Grenfell & the Congo. *v.*2, *pp.*718–24. Hutchinson. 1908.   *i.*
> *Observations on several types of drum, xylo, flute & harp, with notation of Babangi boat song & Bateke dirge : good illust.*

OVERBERGH, CYRILLE van. Les Basonge [Coll. Mon. Ethnog., No. 3] *pp.*359–64. Brux. 1908.
> *Informative notes on singing & instr.*

DELHAISE, CHARLES. Chez les Wasongola du Sud [Soc. R. Belge Géog., 33 : 182–86 : 1909]   *i.*
> *Descr. instr. & singing, with notation of two songs.*

,, Les Warega [Coll. Mon. Ethnog., No. 5] *pp.*269, 271–73. Brux. 1909.
> *Summary of data on instr., with notation of a ' ransambi ' air.*

MAES, JOSEPH. Les Warumbi [Anthropos, Wien, 4 : 627 : 1909]
> *Mention of musical bow, songs & dances.*

OVERBERGH, CYRILLE van. Les Mangbetu [Coll. Mon. Ethnog., No. 4] *pp.*417–22. Brux. 1909.
> *Notes on singing & instr.*

TRILLES, HENRI. Les légendes des Bena Kanioka et le folklore Bantou [Anthropos, Wien, 4 : 950, 954 *et seq.* : 1909]
> *Descr. & illust. of Baluba bow instr. accompanying songs : notation of several folk melodies, with comments.*

WEEKS, JOHN H. Notes on some customs of the Lower Congo people [Folk Lore, 20 : 198, 458–59, 463 *et seq.* : 1909]   *i.*
> *Brief descr. of ' nsambi ', marimba & dance drums.*

BUTAYE, R. Dictionnaire kikongo-français et français-kikongo. *p.*73. Roulers : Meester. 1910.
> *Gives list of musical instr. : see also under* Tambour, *etc.*

TORDAY, EMIL. Land & peoples of Kasai Basin [Geog. Jour., 36 : 30–31 : 1910]
> *Brief descr. of Batetela drum.*

TORDAY, EMIL & JOYCE, THOMAS ATHOL. Notes ethnographiques sur les Bakuba : les Bushonga [Ann. Mus. Congo Belge, Ser. III— Ethnog.] *v.*2, *pt.*1, *pp.*98–104, 269. Brux. 1910.   *i.*
> *Important account of singing & instr., with good illust.*

VIAENE, ERNEST & BERNARD, *** Chez les Lessa [Soc. R. Belge Géog., 34 : 222 : 1910]
> *Incidental mention of instr., professional musicians & songs.*

WARD, HERBERT. A voice from the Congo. *pp.*298–304. N.Y. : Scribner. 1910.   *i.*
> *Informative account of instr. & songs, with notation of two canoe songs.*

WEEKS, JOHN H.   Anthropological notes on the Bangala of the Upper Congo River [R. Anthrop. Inst., 40 : 402–04 : 1910]
Musical abilities of Boloki discussed : singing, drums & rattles.

BITTREMIEUX, LEO.   De geheime Sekte der Bakhimba's.   *pp.*94–100, 171–72.   Leuven : Reekmans.   1911.
Observations on dancing : notation of Mayombe song, compared to plainsong.

COLLE, F.   Les Baluba [Coll. Mon. Ethnog., Nos. 10 & 11]   *pp.*673–91, 699–710.   Brux.   1911.
Notes on Basiba panpipe dance, singing, instr. & children's games : notation of several songs given.

DANIEL, GASTON.   La musique au Congo [S. I. M., Paris, 8 : 56–64 : 1911]
On music, dancing, singing & instr. of Mayombe & Bangala, with notation of five melodies.

ENGELS, *Lieut.*   Les Wangata [Rev. Cong., 3 : 203–06 : 1911]
Descr. of singing, amateur & professional, & the few instr. used.

HALKIN, JOSEPH.   Les Ababua [Coll. Mon. Ethnog., No. 7]   *pp.*249, 427–36.   Brux.   1911.
Summary of data on dances, songs, singing & instr.

„ Quelques peuplades du district de l'Uelé [Mouvements Sociol. Internat., 8 : 109–15 : ?1911]
Observations on dances, songs & instr.

HILTON-SIMPSON, MELVILLE WILLIAM.   Land & peoples of the Kasai. *pp.*35–36, 254–55.   Constable.   1911.
Descr. Bambala flutes & friction drum, Basonge instr. & dancing.

MAES, JOSEPH.   Notes sur quelques objets des Pygmées-Wambuti [Anthropos, Wien, 6 : 135 : 1911]
Brief descr. of sansa.

SELIGMANN, CHARLES GABRIEL.   An Avungura drum [Man, 11 : 17 : 1911]

TORDAY, EMIL.   Der Tofoke [Mitt. Anthrop. Gesell. Wien, 41 : 192–93 : 1911]
Several instr. descr.

CUREAU, ADOLPHE.   Les sociétés primitives de l'Afrique Equatoriale. *pp.*91–96.   Paris : Colin.   1912.
Singing & instr. described, with notation of Azande, Bangala, Banziri, Mobango, Bakongo, Fang, & Yakuma airs.

DELEVAL, H.   Les tribus Kavati du Mayombe [Rev. Cong., 261–62 : 1912]
Notes on instr. & professional musicians.

DELHAISE, CHARLES.   Les Bapopoïe [Soc. R. Belge Géog., 36 : 183–85 : 1912]
Short account of dances & instr., noting absence of singing.

MAES, JOSEPH.   On xylophones of Bakuba [Man, 12 : 90–93 : 1912]   *i. Congo xylophones classified into two kinds : detailed descr. of Bakuba instr.*

55

MAES, JOSEPH. Les tam-tams du Congo Belge. 19*pp.* Louvain : Ceuterick. 1912. *i.*
  Detailed descr. of drums of several types.

„ Xylophones du Congo Belge [Rev. Cong., 116–23 : 1912] *i.*
  Congo xylophones classified into two kinds & into two separated dispersion zones : two common places of origin suggested. Detailed notes on four instr. at Tervueren.

SCHMITZ, ROBERT. Les Baholoholo [Coll. Mon. Ethnog., No. 9] *pp.*407–19, 421–23. Brux. 1912.
  Summary of data on dance music & instr.

STARR, FREDERICK. Congo natives. *See* Plates 1, 18, 19, 43, 46, 48, 49, 61, 123. Chicago : for author. 1912. *i.*
  Good illust. of Baluba musical bows, & drums, rattles & other instr. of Bakongo, Bakete & Bangala.

DELEVAL, HECTOR. Les tribus Kavati du Mayombe. *pp.*50–51. Brux. 1913.
  Brief note on instr.

HARFELD, *le Commandant.* Mentalités indigènes du Katanga [Soc. R. Belge Géog., 37 : 44–45 : 1913]
  Notation of boat– & carriers' songs, & comment thereon.

TORDAY, EMIL. The new Congo collection [Mus. Jour. Phil., 4 : 21–24 : 1913] *i.*
  Notes on marimba, friction-drum & flute, well illust.

WEEKS, JOHN H. Among Congo cannibals. *pp.*92–93, 119. Seeley, Service. 1913.
  Comments on Boloki singing & river songs.

BAEYENS, M. Les Lesa [Rev. Cong., 327–28 : 1914]
  Short notes on improvisation, river songs & instr.

TANGHE, BASIEL. De Slang bij de Ngbandi. *pp.*75–76. Brux. Goemare. 1919.
  Gives notation of three songs.

MAES, JOSEPH. La sanza du Congo Belge [Congo, Brux., 1 : 542–72 : 1921] *i.*
  Details of structure, form & technique of the sanzas of Belgian Congo : with map showing distribution of four types.

PRING, S. W. Music on the Congo [Music Student, 141–42, 1921]
  A brief general article.

CLARIDGE, G. CYRIL. Wild bush tribes of tropical Africa. *pp.*221–46. Seeley, Service. 1922.
  General account of music & instr. of Bakongo.

EMPAIN, A. Les Bakela de la Loto [Soc. R. Belge Géog., 46 : 257–60 : 1922] *i.*
  Notes on gong, globefruit, horns & rattles, & on range of singing.

RUYDANT, F. La musique congolaise [Sélection, Paris, 1 : 69–72 : 1922]
  General remarks on music & singing : with notation of "kansambi" air & boat song.

TORDAY, EMIL & JOYCE, THOMAS ATHOL. Notes ethnographiques sur les populations habitant les bassins du Kasai et du Kwango oriental [Ann. Mus. Congo Belge, Ser. III—Ethnog.] *v.2, pt.2, pp.*18–19, 25, 55–63, 203, 274–78. Brux. 1922. *i.*
> *Important account & detailed descr. of music & instr. of 8 tribes: good illust.*

DARRÉ, E. La tribu Bondjo [Soc. Rech. Cong., 3 : 70 : 1923]
> *Note on instr. & dances.*

HALL, HENRY USHER. Notes on some Congo & West African wood-carvings. [Mus. Jour. Phil., 14 : 101–34 : 1923] *i.*
> *Good illust. (fig.25) of Bayaka slit gong.*

CZEKANOWSKI, JAN. Forschungen im Nil-Kongo-Zwischengebiet. *v.*6, *pt.*2, *pp.*291–93, 382–84, 434–35. Leip. : Klinkhardt. 1924.
> *Notes on Mabudu, Bakondjo & Momvu instr.*

FOCQUET-VANDERKERKEN, *** Les populations indigènes des terri-toires de Kutu et de Nseontin [Congo, Brux., 2 : 170–71 : 1924] *i.*
> *Note on gongs of the Basakata.*

VAN MOL, O. P. Pubertertsviering en besnijdenis bij Mambutu's [Congo, Brux., 1 : 362–74 : 1924]
> *Contains notation of music accompanying circumcision dances.*

DARRÉ, E. & LE BOURHIS, *** Notes sur la tribu Bomitaba [Bul. Soc. Rech. Cong., 5 : 36–37 : 1925]
> *Descr. dances, instr., music & songs.*

TANGHE, J. Chansons de pagayeurs [Congo, Brux., 2 : 206–14 : 1927]
,, Ditto. [Sch. Orient. Stud., 4 : 827–38 : 1928]
> *Good analysis & notation of seventeen Mabale river-songs from phonog. recordings & discussion of these.*

FORRER, RAYMOND. La géographie musicale du Congo Belge [L'Expansion Belge, Brux., 33–34 : 1928]
> *A general article on distribution of instr.*

SCHUMACHER, *le R. P.* Les pygmées Bagêsêra et Bazigaba aux Cascades du Karambo-Bikore [Congo, Brux., 1 : 177–79 : 1928] *i.*
> *Brief descr. of a stringed instr. : note on nature of African scale.*

VERBEKEN, A. L. Etude sur la peuplade des Bombesa [Soc. R. Belge Géog., 52 : 72 : 1928]
> *Contains notation of one song, & note on instr.*

MAES, JOSEPH. Un tam-tam d'initiation du Haut Kwilu [Man, 29 : 167–69 : 1929] *i.*
> *Short descr. of ritual drums.*

TANGHE, BASIEL. De ziel van het Ngbandivolk [Congo Bibliothek] *pp.*95–97, *et seq.* Brugge : De Gruuthuuse Persen. 1929.
> *Note on several instr., singing & songs.*

,, De Ngbandi naar het leven geschetst [Congo Bibliothek] *pp.*9–12, 210–17. Brugge : De Gruuthuuse Persen. [1929?] *i.*
> *Informative notes on instr., harmony, & songs.*

FRANCK, LOUIS. Le Congo Belge. *v.*1, *pp.*368–69 : *v.*2, *pp.*417–20. Brux. : La Renaissance du Livre. 1930. *i.*
> *Very general remarks on Congo music, chiefly derivative.*

PLANCQUAERT, M. Les sociétés secrètes chez les Bayaka. Figures 4, 17, 24, 26–29, 30–33. Brux. : Falk. 1930. *i*.
> *Good illust. of dancing & drumming.*

BERNATZIK, H. A. The Dark Continent. Studio, Ltd. 1931.
> *See excellent illust. of Niambara flute-player.*

SCHEBESTA, PAUL. Bambuti, die Zwerge vom Kongo. *pp.*25, 65–66, 96–97, 182–83, 234–37, 244. Leip. : Brockhaus. 1932. *i*.
> *Scattered references to instr., singing, pan-flute dance : good illust. of musical bows, flutes & zithers.*

SERVATIUS, le R. P. De besnijdenis bij de Bene Nsamba [Anthropos, Wien, 27 : 526, 529, 532 : 1932]
> *Short notes on dances, drums & singing.*

VAN MOL, O. P. Het huwelijk bij de Mambutu's [Congo, Brux., 2 : 207–11 : 1932]
> *Contains music of dances at marriage ceremonies : with notation.*

IMMENROTH, WILHELM. Kultur und Umwelt der Kleinwüchsigen in Afrika [Studien zur Völkerkunde, 6. *pp.*134–37, 271–74. Leip. 1933]
> *Brief account of pygmy & Bushman dancing, singing & instr.*

TRILLES, HENRI. Les Pygmées de la forêt équatoriale. *pp.*331–60. Paris : Bloud & Gay. 1933.
> *Good & detailed notes on singing, instr. & dancing. See also Index : " Chant ". Notation of several songs given.*

CLOSSON, ERNEST. La musique indigène congolaise. *In* Cinquante années d'activité coloniale au Congo, 1885–1935. *pp.*296–97. Brux. : L'Avenir Belge. 1935.
> *A brief survey only.*

ANTHEIL, GEORGE. [Bacongo songs] *In* Negro anthology, ed. Nancy Cunard. *pp.*419–20. Wishart. 1934.
> *Gives notation of several melodies.*

CLYMANS, ROLAND. Boula Matari : musique folklorique du Congo Belge. 14*pp.* Brux. : Dogilbert. 1934.

SCHEBESTA, PAUL. Vollblutneger und Halbzwerge. 263*pp.* Salzburg : Rustet. 1934. *i*.
> *See index : scattered references to Trommeln. Good illust. of flute ensemble, harp, band & zither, figures 58, 94, 23 & 21 respectively.*

THOMAS, JEAN. A travers l'Afrique équatoriale sauvage. *pp.*16, 17, 46, 47, 49, 59, 76–77. Paris : Larose. 1934. *i*.
> *Scattered notes on singing, with notation of several Bateke & Thali river songs.*

HULSTAERT, GUSTAAF. Notes sur les instr. de musique à l'Equateur [Congo, Brux., 2 : 184–200, et seq. : 1935] *i*.
> *Describes in some detail instr. of Batwa & several other Congo tribes.*

19—RUANDA-URUNDI

VAN der BURGT, JEAN MARTIN MICHEL. Dictionnaire Français-Kirundi. Bois le Duc : L'Illustration Catholique. 1903.
> *See headings : chant, musicien, danse, hymne.*

Van der Burgt, Jean Martin Michel. Un grand peuple de l'Afrique équatoriale. *pp.*20–21, 91–93. Bois le Duc : L'Illustration Catholique. 1903. *i.*

   Notes on instr. & singing of Barundi.

Dufays, Félix. Lied und Gesang bei Brautwerbung und Hochzeit in Mulera-Ruanda [Anthropos, Wien, 4 : 847–78 : 1909]

   Incidental references to music at tribal festivals, with notation of five tunes.

Schumacher, *** Die Ehe in Ruanda [Anthropos, Wien, 5 : 897–906 : 1910]

   Scattered information about rhythm and form of Bahutu & Batutsi songs, with four pages of notation.

Arnoux, Alex. Le culte de la Société secrète des Imándwa au Ruanda [Anthropos, Wien, 7 : 546–51, 852–74 ; 1912 : & 8 : 111–12 : 1913]

   Contains occasional references to ritual songs, with notation and comments.

Meyer, Hans. Die Barundi. *pp.*65–70, 158. Leip. ; Spämer. 1916. *i.*

   Notes on dances, instr., songs and singing.

Hornbostel, Erich M. von. Gesänge aus Ruanda. *In* Czekanowski, Jan : Wissenschaftliche Ergebnisse der Deutschen Zentral-Afrika-Expedition, 1907–08. *v.*6, *pt.*1, *pp.*379–412, & append. Leip. : Klinkhardt. 1917.

   Important analysis of 43 songs from phonog. recordings, with detailed discussion : Bahutu, Batutsi & Batwa.

Belgium—Ministère des Colonies. Rapport sur l'administration belge du Ruanda et de l'Urundi pendant l'année 1926. *p.*102. Brux. [?1927]

   Note on the manufacture of native drums.

Zuure, Bernard. L'âme du Murundi. *pp.*452–56. Paris : Beauchesne. 1932.

   General remarks on Barundi music (from Hornbostel, etc.) : parallel of Gregorian chant examined.

,, Poésies chez les Barundi [Africa, 5 : 344–54 : 1932]

   Note on relation between poetry, music & dance : notation of one melody given.

20—UGANDA

Speke, John Hanning. Journal of the discovery of the source of the Nile. *pp.*212, 255. Blackwood. 1863. *i.*

   Observations on Baganda, Wanyambo & Wahuma instr.

Grant, *Lt.-Col.* James Augustus. A walk across Africa. *pp.*103–04, 182–85. Blackwood. 1864.

   Descr. of Baganda flute.

Wilson, Charles Thomas & Felkin, Robert William. Uganda & the Egyptian Sudan. *v.*1, *pp.*154–57, 214–16 ; *v.*2, *p.*132. Sampson Low. 1882.

   Descr. Baganda instr. & singing.

STUHLMANN, FRANZ.   Mit Emin Pascha ins Herz von Afrika.   *pp.*178, 324 (note).   Berl. : Reimer.   1894.   *i.*
  Descr. instr. of Baganda & Banyoro.

KOLLMANN, PAUL.   Der Nordwesten unserer Ostafrikanischen Kolonie· pp.25–27.   Berl. : Schall.   1898.   *i.*
  Notes on instr. of Baganda.

„ The Victoria Nyanza.   pp.37–39.   Swan, Sonnenschein.   1899.   *i.*
  Instr. of Baganda descr.

SCHOELLER, MAX.   Mitteilungen über meine Reise nach Äquatorial Ostafrika und Uganda, 1896–97.   *v.*2, *p.*306.   Berl. : Reimer. 1901.   *i.*
  Kavirondo instr. descr.   See also index to illust. in v.2.

HOBLEY, CHARLES WILLIAM.   Eastern Uganda : an ethnological survey [R. Anthrop. Inst. Occasional Papers I] *pp.*19–20, 30, 38.   1902.   *i.*
  Mention of Kavirondo reed harps & drums.

JOHNSTON, *Sir* HARRY HAMILTON.   The Uganda Protectorate.   *pp.*210, 558, 664–66, 697, 778, 834, 851.   Hutchinson.   1902.   *i.*
  Discusses Egyptian influence on instr. : note on Baganda & Masai instr. & singing, with notation of xylo air & Suk melody.

CASTELLANI, ALDO & MOCHI, ALDOBRANDINO.   Contributo all' antropologia dell'Uganda [R. Soc. Geog. Ital., 41 : 1087–89 : 1904]
  Kavirondo & Baganda drums, flutes & stringed instr. descr. ; from examples in Museo Nazionale, etc.

POWELL–COTTON, PERCY HORACE GORDON.   In unknown Africa. *pp.*228, 236–37, 316.   Hurst.   1904.   *i.*
  Contains short account of Kavirondo band.

CUNNINGHAM, J. FRANCIS.   Uganda & its peoples.   *pp.*92, 289–90. Hutchinson.   1905.
  Notes on Basiba & Lake islanders' flute dances & harps.

MELDON, JAMES AUSTIN.   Notes on the Bahima of Ankole [Jour. Afr. Soc., 6 : 239 : 1907]   *i.*
  Brief note on stringed instr., drum & bell.

„ Notes on the Sudanese in Uganda [Jour. Afr. Soc., 7 : 142–43 : 1907]   *i.*
  Note on horn & lyre.

ROSCOE, JOHN.   The Bahima : a cow tribe of Enkole [R. Anthrop. Inst., 37 : 117 : 1907]
  Brief note on songs & harps.

JOHNSON, T. BROADWOOD.   Tramps round the Mountains of the Moon. *p.*242.   Fisher Unwin.   1908.   *i.*
  Illust. of Busoga harp.

WEISS, MAX.   Die .Völkerstämme in Norden Deutsch–Ostafrikas. *pp.*54, 112, 145–47, 237–40, 298–99, 308, 314–16.   Berl. : Marschner. 1910.
  Descr. notes on instr. of Bahutu, Bakulia, Wageia & Wanyambe.

ROSCOE, JOHN.   The Baganda.   *pp.*25–37.   Macmillan.   1911.
  Excellent notes on drums & their tribal functions.

KITCHING, ARTHUR LEONARD.   On the backwaters of the Nile.   *pp.*228, 234–35, 255.   Fisher Unwin.   1912.   *i.*
> *Brief account of Gan' harps, with notation of flute solo.*

ROSCOE, JOHN.   The Northern Bantu.   *pp.*87–88, 140, 189.   Camb. : U. P.   1915.
> *Short notes on ritual drums, harps, zithers & songs.*

DRIBERG, JOHN HERBERT.   A preliminary account of the Didinga [Sudan Notes & Records, Khartoum, 5 : 222 : 1922]
> *Note on sacred drums & harps : mentions absence of instr. at dances.*

STIGLER, ROBERT.   Einige wenig bekannte Volksstämme Ugandas [Mitt. Anthrop. Gesell. Wien, 52 : 237–38 : 1922]
> *Brief notes on Bagesu guitars & lyre.*

ROSCOE, JOHN.   The Bakitara of Banyoro.   *pp.*112–13, 230–31.   Camb. : U. P.   1923.   *i.*
> *Notes on manufacture & use of drums.   See also index : Drums.*

ROSCOE, JOHN.   The Banyankole.   *pp.*44 *et seq.*, 81, 95.   Camb.: U. P. 1923.   *i.*
> *Brief descr. of drums & rattles.*

DRIBERG, JOHN HERBERT.   The Lango.   *pp.*87–88, 123–30.   Fisher Unwin.   1923.
> *Informative account of manufacture & use of drums : note on scale, with descr. of flutes & two obsolescent instr.*

ROSCOE, JOHN.   The Bagesu.   *pp.*193 *et seq.*   Camb. : U. P.   1924.
> *Note on kinds of drum & mention of other instr.*

SHAY, FELIX.   Fife & drum corps of a Uganda chief [Nat. Geog. Mag., 47 : 174, 181, 189, 191 : 1925]   *i.*
> *Good illust. of Toro instr.*

X.Y.Z., *pseud.* [i.e. J. M. DUNCAN]   Native music [Uganda Jour., 1 : 63 : 1934]
> *General remarks on need for scientific data about Baganda music.*

LUSH, ALLAN J.   Kiganda drums [Uganda Jour., 3 : 7–25 : 1925]   *i.*
> *Good account of manufacture, use & social significance of many types of drum.*

MOLINARO, L.   I Didinga, tribù dell'Africa Orientale [Anthropos, Wien, 30 : 425 : 1935]
> *Instr. briefly descr.*

KAGWA, *Sir* APOLO.   The customs of the Baganda [ed. by M. Mandelbaum Edel] [Columbia Univ.   Contributions to Anthrop., *v.*22] *pp.*140–49.   N.Y.   1934.
> *Notes on songs, instr. & their tribal significance.*

21—KENYA

FISCHER, G. A.   Das Wapokomo-Land und seine Bewohner [Mitt. Geog. Gesell. Hamburg, 30–32 ; 1878–79]
> *Descr. of drum : notes on singing & dancing, with notation of two melodies.*

HINDE, SIDNEY LANGFORD & HINDE, HILDEGARDE. The last of the
Masai. *p.*37. Heinemann. 1901.
Note on form of songs.

MERKER, M. Die Masai. *pp.*122–23. Berl. : Reimer. 1904.
Brief note on songs, with notation of one melody.

HOLLIS, *Sir* ALFRED CLAUDE. The Nandi : their language and folklore.
*pp.*39–40, 87, 277. Oxf. : Clarendon Press. 1909.
Horns, friction-drums & other instr. descr. with vernacular names.

HOBLEY, CHARLES WILLIAM. Ethnology of A-Kamba & other East
African tribes [Camb. Archaeol. Ethnog. Ser.] *pp.*32–33. Camb. :
U. P. 1910.
Notes on harp, pipes, horns & whistles, & various kinds of drums.

ROUTLEDGE, WILLIAM SCORESBY & ROUTLEDGE, KATHERINE. With
a prehistoric people : the Akikuyu of British East Africa. *pp.*111–
15. Arnold. 1910.
*Notes on singing & instr., with analysis & notation of six songs
from phonog. recordings by C. S. Myers.*

HOBLEY, CHARLES WILLIAM. Further researches into Kikuyu &
Kamba religious beliefs & customs [R. Anthrop. Inst., 41 : 439
et seq. : 1911]
" Gourd of song " descr.

WERNER, ALICE. Note on ' fufuriye ' flutes [Jour. Afr. Soc., 13 :
102–03 : 1913]

„ Some notes on the Wapokomo of the Tana valley [Jour. Afr. Soc.,
12 : 375–76 : 1913]
Brief descr. of ritual flutes & drums.

SKENE, R. Arab & Swahili dances & ceremonies [R. Anthrop. Inst.,
47 : 413–34 : 1917]
Good descr. of drums & other instr.

LINDBLOM, GERHARD. The Akamba in British East Africa. [Archives
d'études orientales, v.17] *pp.*398–417. *2nd. ed.* Uppsala. 1920.
Useful notes on instr., dancing & singing.

VAN den BERGH, LEONARD JOHN. On the trail of the pigmies.
*pp.*35–36, 64–65. N. Y. : McCann. [1921] *i.*
Brief account of dance instr. & singing.

BROWNE, GRANVILLE ST. JOHN ORDE. The vanishing tribes of Kenya.
*pp.*167–72. Seeley, Service. 1925.
General account of music, instr. & singing.

OLIVER, RICHARD A. C. The musical talent of natives of East Africa
[Brit. Jour. Psychol., genl. sect., 22 : 333–43 : 1932]
*Gives results of psychological tests showing Afr. superiority over
Europeans in sense of intensity, time & rhythm, & inferiority in
sense of pitch, consonance & memory for tones.*

CAGNOLO, C. The Akikuyu. *pp.*161–74. Nyeri : Mission Printing
School. 1933. *i.*
Descr. instr., & form & social significance of songs.

WORTHINGTON, STELLA & WORTHINGTON, E. BARTON. Inland waters
of Africa. *pp.*233–41. Macmillan. 1933.
Discussion of singing, songs & rhythm of the Turkana, with notation.

LINDBLOM, GERHARD. Kamba riddles, proverbs & songs [Archives d'études orientales, v.20. pt.3] *pp.*39–59. Uppsala. 1934.
  Contains notes on text & nature of songs & accompanying instr.
TAYLOR, W. H. Bantu music in Kenya [Oversea Educ., 5 : 168–72 : 1934]
  Discussion of nature of music & singing & European influences thereon.

22—TANGANYIKA

BURTON, *Sir* RICHARD FRANCIS. The Lake regions of Central Africa. *v.*2, *pp.*98, 291–95. Longmans. 1860. *i.*
  Incidental remarks on music & instr.
GRANT, JAMES AUGUSTUS. A walk across Africa. *pp.*182–85. Blackwood. 1864.
  Notes on Karagwe & Wanyembe instr.
JACQUES, VICTOR & STORMS, EMILE. Notes sur l'ethnographie de la partie orientale de l'Afrique équatoriale. *pp.*37–45. Brux. Hayez. 1886. *i.*
„ *Ditto* [Bul. Soc. Anthrop. Brux., 5 : 127–35 : 1886] *i.*
  Notes on dances, instr. & songs of several tribes.
PFEIL, *Graf* JOACHIM. Beobachtungen Während meiner letzten Reise in Ostafrika [Petermanns Mitt., 34 : 7–8 : 1888]
  On singing & instr., with notation of xylophone air.
BAUMANN, OSCAR. Usambara und seine Nachbargebiete. *pp.*50–55, 136–38, 350–53. Berl. : Reimer. 1891.
  Good account of Swahili & Wabondei instr., with notation of 22 Swahili airs.
„ Durch Massailand zur Nilquelle. *pp.* 202, 224, 232. Berl. : Reimer. 1894. *i.*
  Brief notes on instr. of Washashi, Wanyamwesi & Barundi.
HERRMANN, *** Die Wasiba und ihr Land [Mitt. Schutz, 7 : 51 : 1894]
  Instr. briefly enumerated.
STUHLMANN, FRANZ. Mit Emin Pascha ins Herz von Afrika. *pp.*37, 90, 521, 537, 723–24. Berl. : Reimer. 1894. *i.*
  Brief notes on instr. of Twadoë & Wanyamwesi.
KOLLMANN, PAUL. Der Nordwesten unserer Ostafrikanischen Kolonie. *pp.*42, 66–70, 82–83, 115–16, 148–49. Berl. : Schall. 1898. *i.*
  Instr. of Basiba, Wassindja, Wasukuma & Washashi descr.
WERTHER, C. WALDEMAR. Die mittleren Hochländer des nördlichen Deutsch-Ost-Afrikas. *pp.*340, 361, 374. Berl. : Paetel. 1898. *i.*
  Instr. of Sandawa, Wambugwe, Wanyaturu briefly descr. by F. von Luschan.
KOLLMANN, PAUL. The Victoria Nyanza. *pp.*60–61, 94–98, 116, 161–64, 205–08. Swan, Sonnenschein. 1899. *i.*
  Notes on instr. of Basiba, Wassindja, Wasukuma, & Washashi.
WIDENMANN, A. Die Kilimandscharo-Bevölkerung. *pp.*85–86. Gotha : Perthes. 1899.
  Note on Dschagga instr. & trumpet call.

STERN, RUDOLF. Lieder und Sagesweisen und Geschichten der Wanyamwezi [Mitt. Sem. Orient. Sprach. Afr. Stud., 4 : 45-62 : 1901]
Notes on text of songs & accompanying instr.

HOSSFELD, CARL. Ein Beitrag zur ostafrikanischer Lyrik [Globus, Braunschweig, 88 : 82–83 : 1905]
Gives notation of 4 Swahili melodies, & notes on singing.

FÜLLEBORN, FRIEDERICH. Das Deutsche Njassa- und Ruwuma-Gebiet. *pp.*165, 234–42, 338, 458, 554–55. Berl. : Reimer. 1906. *i.*
Good notes on songs, drums, instr. & dance music : see also index : Gesänge, Tanzmusik.

FABRY, HERMANN. Aus dem Leben der Wapogoro [Globus, Braunschweig, 91 : 218–19 : 1907]
Brief account of drums & dance music.

KRAUSS, H. Spielzug der Suahelikinder [Globus, Braunschweig, 92 : 357–59 : 1907] *i.*
Short descr. of children's instr.

WEULE, KARL. Wissenschaftliche Ergebnisse meiner ethnographischen Forschungsreise in den Sud-Osten Deutsch-Ostafrikas [Mitt. Schutz., Erganz. 1 : 95–96 : 1908] *i.*
Instr. of Makua & Makonde descr., & illust. (plates 27–30)

HORNBOSTEL, ERICH M. von. Wanyamwezi-Gesänge [Anthropos, Wien, 4 : 684–701, 919–30 : 1909]
Important discussion on form, rhythm, harmony, etc. of songs, with detailed analysis of fourteen songs from phonog. recordings : several instr. descr.

WEULE, KARL. Native life in East Africa. *pp.*171–72, 264–65, 289–91, 388–92. Pitman. 1909.
Descr. instr. & gives notation of several Wanyamwezi songs from phonog. recordings. See E. M. von Hornbostel's disclaimer of these transcriptions in Globus, 94 : 308 : 1908.

HORNBOSTEL, ERICH M. von. Gesang der Wasukuma [Bul. Acad. Sci. Cracovie : Sciences Naturelles, 711–13 : 1910]
Detailed analysis of seven tunes from phonog. recordings & discussion thereon.

REHSE, HERMANN. Kiziba, Land und Leute. *pp.*65–74. Stuttgart : Strecker. 1910.
Notes on drums & instr., scale & singing of Basiba, with notation of six songs.

WEISS, MAX. Die Völkerstämme in Norden Deutsch-Ostafrikas. *pp.*54, 112, 145–47, 237–40, 298–99, 308, 314–16. Berl. : Marschner. 1910.
Descr. instr. of Bahutu, Bakulia, Wageia & Wanyambe.

CLAUS, HEINRICH. Die Wagogo [Baessler Archiv, Leip., 2 : 36 : 1911]
Brief account of two instr.

JAEGER, FRITZ. Das Hochland der Riesenkrater und die umliegenden Hochländer Deutsch-Ostafrikas [Mitt. Schutz., Erganz. 4 : 100–01 : 1911]
> Describes dances & accompanying songs & instr., with notation of several motifs.

KARÁSEK, A. & EICHHORN, AUGUST. Beiträge zur Kenntnis der Waschambaa, pt.1 [Baessler Archiv, Leip., 1 : 184–85 : 1911]
> Short account of musical bow & friction drum.

LECHAPTOIS, Mgr. Aux rives du Tanganyika. pp.222–32. Alger. 1913.
> Descr. singing & songs of the Wabendi & Wafipa.

MOLITOR, H. La musique chez les nègres du Tanganyika [Anthropos, Wien, 8 : 714–35 : 1913]
> Contains notation of 42 songs from phonog recordings, & discussion thereon, with notes on instr.

RECHE, OTTO. Zur Ethnographie des abflusslosen Gebietes Deutsch-Ostafrikas [Abh. Hamburger Kol. Inst., 17] pp.19, 65, 89–91, 100. Hamburg. 1914. i.
> Brief notes on instr. & singing of Kindija & Wanyaturu.

SICK, EBERHARD V. Die Waniaturu [Baessler Archiv, Leip., 5 : 22 : 1915]
> Short note on stringed instr. & dancing.

WERTH, EMIL. Das deutsch-ostafrikanische Küstenland. v.1, pp.271–74. Berl. : Reimer. 1915.
> Observations on many instr., notation of dance melody & discussion on text & form of songs.

DEMPWOLFF, OTTO. Die Sandawa [Abh. Hamburger Kol. Inst., 34] pp.102–03. Hamburg. 1916.
> Short account of instr. & song, giving dance rhythms.

KARÁSEK, A. & EICHHORN, AUGUST. Beiträge zur Kenntnis der Waschambaa, pt.3 [Baessler Archiv, Leip., 7 : 61–68 : 1918] i.
> Good detailed descr. & illust. of instr.

HAGEMANN, CARL. Spiele der Völker. pp.13–24. Berl. : Schuster. 1919.
> Incidental remarks on music accompanying dances.

ROSCOE, JOHN. Twenty-five years in East Africa. pp.55, 156–57. Camb. : U. P. 1921. i.
> Descr. instr. & songs of Wanyamwezi & other tribes.

MACKENZIE, D. R. The spirit-ridden Konde. pp.160–61. Seeley, Service. 1925.
> Notes on dances & accompanying instr.

KOOTZ-KRETSCHMER, ELISE. Die Safwa. v.1, pp.124–38. Berl. : Reimer. 1926.
> Useful descr. of dances & accompanying songs & instr., showing method of playing.

SPELLIG, FRITZ. Die Wanjamwezi : ein Beitrag zur Völkerkunde Ostafrikas [Zeit. f. Ethnol., 59 : 250–51 : 1927]
> Note on music & instr.

WEBER, WOLFGANG. Negermusik : eine Urform der Unsrigen ? [Die Musik, Berl., 19 : 697–702 : 1927]   *i.*
> *General discussion of melody, rhythm & harmony, with (secondary) notation of Dschagga songs.*

HEINITZ, WILHELM. Lied aus Dar es Salaam transkribiert. *In* Festchrift Heinrich Wilhelm Augustin. Glückstadt. 1932.

KOHN, *** West and East African songs. *In* Negro Anthology, ed. Nancy Cunard. *pp.*416–18. Wishart. 1934.
> *Contains notation of three airs from phonog. recordings.*

CULWICK, A. T. & CULWICK, G. M. Ubena of the Rivers.   *pp.*401–12. Allen & Unwin. 1935. *i.*
> *Chapter on song & dance, with good descr. of drums, flute, rattles.*

CULWICK, A. T. A Pogoro flute [Man, 35 : 40 : 1935]   *i.*

CÉSARD, EDMOND. Le Muhaya. viii. Les arts : musique, danse, jeux [Anthropos, Wien, 31 : 489–93 : 1936]
> *Descr. several instr., with vernacular names.*

23—NYASALAND

JOHNSTON, *Sir* HARRY HAMILTON. British Central Africa.   *pp.*460, 464–68. Methuen. 1897. *i.*
> *Account of Yao instr., singing, & drum manufacture.*

WERNER, ALICE. The natives of British Central Africa [Native Races of the British Empire] *pp.*216–29. Constable. 1906. *i.*
> *General remarks on songs & brief descr. of instr., with good illust.*

STIGAND, CHAUNCEY HUGH. Notes on the natives of Nyassaland, North East Rhodesia & Portuguese Zambesia [R. Anthrop. Inst., 37 : 129–30 : 1907] *i.*
> *Note on instr. & singing of Angoni.*

WEULE, KARL. Native life in East Africa. *pp.*171–72. Pitman. 1909.
> *Short notes on Yao music.*

STANNUS, HUGH STANNUS. Notes on some tribes of British Central Africa [R. Anthrop. Inst., 40 : 333–34 : 1910]
> *Brief note on instr. accompanying dances.*

 „ A rare type of musical instr. from Central Africa [Man, 20 : 37–39 : 1920] *i.*
> *Good descr. & illust. of a Nyanja gourd drum.*

KIDNEY, ELLA. Native songs from Nyasaland [Jour. Afr. Soc., 20 : 116–26 : 1921]
> *Notes on Chikundu singing, tonality, drum-making, instr. : see additional discussion, pp.*140–41.

 „ Songs of Nyasaland [Outward Bound, 1/7 : 31–37 ; & 1/12 : 23–29, 74 : 1921]
> *Notes on singing, drum-making & songs, with notation of two airs, " harmonised ".*

STANNUS, HUGH STANNUS. The Wayao of Nyasaland [Harvard Afr. Stud., 3] *pp.*365–70. Cambridge, Mass. 1922. *i.*
> *Good detailed description of Yao instr. : notes on songs & dances.*

HOLLAND, THEODORE. Songs from Nyasaland ; tunes collected and
text translated by Ella J. Kidney. 25*pp.* Curwen. 1924.
  *Consists of notation of "arranged" airs : of little scientific
  importance.*
WERNER, ALICE. On a stringed instr. obtained at Ntumbi, Nyasaland,
in 1894 [Bantu Stud., 5 : 257–58 : 1931]
YOUNG, T. CULLEN. Notes on the customs & folklore of the Tumbuka-
Kamanga peoples. *p.*87. Livingstonia : Mission Press. 1931.
  Short description of a reed-dance & marriage-dances.
HERZOG, GEORGE. African songs of the Chewa tribe in British East
Africa. *In* Negro anthology, ed. Nancy Cunard. *pp.*412–14.
Wishart. 1934.
  *Informative & general remarks on Afr. music, with notation of
  several songs from phonog. recordings.*
„ Speech-melody & primitive music [Music Quart., 20 : 452–66 : 1934]
  Includes notation of Chewa airs from phonog. records.
M[OSELEY], A. B. More about music [Cent. Afr., 52 : 54–55 : 1934]
  Gives notation of canoe songs from phonog. recordings, with discussion.

24—ZANZIBAR

BURTON, *Sir* RICHARD FRANCIS. Zanzibar. *v.*1, *pp.*430–31 ; *v.*2,
*pp.*91–92, 137. Tinsley. 1872.
  Gives list of Swahili instr., & descr. of Muansa drums.
SCHMIDT, KARL WILHELM. Sansibar. *pp.*75–78. Leip. : Brockhaus.
1888. *i.*
  Descr. & illust. of drums, kinanda & other instr.
PRUEN, S. TRISTRAM. The Arab & the African. *pp.*99–103. Seeley,
Service. 1891.
  *General remarks on instr. & chorus singing, with notation of chants
  & Wanyamwezi airs.*
SACLEUX, CHARLES. Dictionnaire français-swahili. *p.*645. Zanzibar :
Miss. des Pères du St. Esprit. 1891.
  List of instr. under headings : Musicien, Musique, Tambour.
ROSE, ALGERNON S. African primitive instr. [Pro. Music. Assn.,
1903–04 : 91–108 : 1904]
  Descr. several Zanzibar instr.
ANON. Les instruments de musique en usage à Zanzibar [Rev. Music.,
6 : 165–68 : 1906] *i.*
  Brief comments on drums & stringed instr.
WERTH, EMIL. Das deutsch-ostafrikanische Küstenland. *v.*1, *pp.*271–74.
Berl. : Reimer. 1915.
  Notes on Pemba instr. & songs.
INGRAMS, WILLIAM HAROLD. *In* Zanzibar : an account of its people,
industries & history. [British Empire Exhibition, Wembley, 1924]
*pp.*12–14. 1924.
  Short account of songs, instr. & dances.
„ Zanzibar. *pp.*399–420. Witherby. 1931.
  *Good account of instr., dances & accompanying music, with
  notation of several songs.*

SALT, HENRY. Voyage to Abyssinia, 1809–10. *pp.*41–42, 380–81, 447. Rivington. 1814. *i.*
Notes on music of " Makooas ".

MONTEIRO, ROSE. Delagoa Bay : its natives & natural history. *pp.*250–53. Philip. 1891.
Goura & other instr. descr. : notes on Chobi songs.

MÜLLER, HENDRIK PIETER NICOLAAS & SNELLEMAN, JOH. F. Industrie des Cafres du Sudest de l'Afrique. *pp.*46–47 & *appendix.* Leiden : Brill. 1893. *i.*
Brief descr. of instr. (see plates 21–23) : gives notation of six songs.

JEANNERET, PHILIPPE. Les Ma-Khoça [Soc. Neuchât. Géog., 8 : 137 : 1895] *i.*
Brief note on instr.

JUNOD, HENRI ALEXANDRE. Les chants et les contes des Ba-Ronga. *pp.*5–66. Lausanne : Bridel. 1897. *i.*
Good account of songs, with notation from phonog. recordings, & illust. & scale of marimba.

„ Les Baronga. *pp.*24, 26, 50, 112, 131, 146, 171, 263–77, 419, 445. Neuchâtel : Attinger. 1898.
*Useful notes on songs & instr., with notation of several melodies : also published in Bul. Soc. Neuchât. Geog., v.*10, 1898.

MAUGHAM, REGINALD CHARLES FULKE. Portuguese East Africa. *pp.*286–88. Murray. 1906. *i.*
Brief notes on instr.

BARRETT, JOHN O.W. Impressions & scenes of Mozambique [Nat. Geog. Mag., 21b : 819–22, 828–29 : 1910] *i.*
Good illust. of marimba & drum orchestras.

CABRAL, AUGUSTO. Raças, usos e costumes dos indigenas do districto de Inhambane. *pp.*109–15. Lourenço Marques : Imprensa Nacional. 1910. *i.*
Good detailed descr. of drums, marimbas, songs & dances.

JUNOD, HENRI ALEXANDRE. The life of a South African tribe. *v.*1, *pp.*403–04 ; *v.*2, *pp.*248–69, 441 *et seq.* Macmillan. 1912. *i.*
„ *Ditto.* *v.*1, *p.*431 ; *v.*2, *pp.*276–300, 423, 484. Macmillan. 1928. *i.*
Important discussion of Thonga musical characteristics, & descr. of instr.

CURTIS, NATALIE BURLIN. Songs & tales from the Dark Continent. *pp.*81–129. N.Y. : Schirmer. 1920.
Gives notation of Chindau rain-, spirit-, love-, & dance-songs.

SACADURA, FERNANDO de. Usos e costumes de Quiteve [Bol. Soc. Geog. Lisboa, 46 : 369–72 : 1928]
Instr. accompanying dances descr.

SANTOS RUFINO, JOSÉ dos. Albuns fotográficos e descritivos . . . da . . . colónia de Moçambique. *v.*10, *p.*30. Hamburg : Broschek. 1929. *i.*
Illust. of marimba & drum band.

IDELSOHN, A. Z. Musical characteristics of Eastern European Jewish folksong [Music. Quart., 18 : 634–45 : 1932]
Contains notation of three songs by natives of Portuguese East Africa at Johannesburg.

EARTHY, E. DORA. VaLenge women : social & economic life. *pp.*96, 172–81, 209–10. Milford. 1933.
Good notes on dances, drums & other instr., with notation of one melody.

JORGE, TOMÁS. As aptidões musicais dos indígenas de Moçambique [Bol. Soc. Estudos Moçambique, 3 : 163–84 : 1934]
Contains eight pages of notation.

JUNOD, HENRI ALEXANDRE. Vier afrikanische Spiele. 56*pp.* Zurich : Wanderer-Verlag. ? 1934.
Native themes dramatised : Thonga tunes are incorporated.

JUNOD, HENRI PHILIPPE. Les cas de possession et l'exorcisme chez les Vandau [Africa, 7 : 275–99 : 1934]
Gives notation of four ritual songs.

KIRBY, PERCIVAL R. The musical instr. of the native races of S. Africa. *pp.*57–65. Milford. 1934. *m. & i.*
Excellent account of Chopi instr. & music.

BASTOS, MARIA HENRIQUETA CALÇADA. Tres canções dos Maputo [Moçambique, Lourenço Marques, 2 : 29–40 : 1935] *i.*
Informative discussion of historical songs, with notation.

BASTOS, MARIA HENRIQUETA CALÇADA & MONTEZ, C. Canções Djongas (Magude) [Moçambique, Lourenço Marques, 3 : 17–29 : 1935] *i.*
Songs & accompanying instr. described & illust., with notation.

„ Kossi n'quaio ! . . . A grande festa do rei Gungunhana [Moçambique, Lourenço Marques, 4 : 5–24 : 1935] *i.*
Describes festival dances, with notation of two choruses.

JUNOD, HENRI PHILIPPE. The Vathonga [Bantu Tribes of S. Afr., *v.*4, section 1] Plate 39. Camb. : Deighton Bell. 1935. *i.*
Musical bow well illust.

„ The Vachopi of Port. E. Africa [Bantu Tribes of S. Afr. *v.*4, Section 2] *p.*48, & plates 70–73. Camb. : Deighton Bell. 1936. *i.*
Good illust. of xylos being played & Chopi orchestra.

26—ANGOLA

MONTECUCCULO, A. CAVAZZI da. Istorica descrittione de tre regni Congo, Matamba et Angola. *pp.* 133–34. Milano : Agnelli. 1690. *i.*
*Good detailed descr. of instr. : see interesting plates, pp.*127, 142 *& 158.*

MEROLLA da SORRARTO, GIROLAMO. Breve e succinta relatione del viaggio nel Congo. *pp.*170–73. Napoli : Mollo. 1692. *i.*

„ A voyage to Congo, 1692. [Pinkerton's Voyages, 10 : 244–45 : 1814]
Good descr. & illust. of marimba & several other instr. of Ambundu.

ZUCCHELLI, ANTONIO. Merckwürdige Missions und Reisebeschreibung nach Congo in Ethiopien. *pp.*173–74, 195. Frankfurt-a-M. 1715.
Describing Loanda instr. & drums.

LABAT, JEAN BAPTISTE. Relation historique de l'Ethiopie occidentale. *v.*1, *pp.*246, 248, 398 ; *v.*2, *pp.*48–56. Paris : Delespine. 1732. *i.*
Contains descr. of instr. from Montecucculo (supra).

MAGYAR, LADISLAUS. Reisen in Sudafrika. *v.*1, *pp.*311–14. Pest : Lauffer. 1859. *i.*
Descr. marimba & other instr. of Ambundu : see plates at end.

VALDEZ, FRANCISCO TRAVASSOS. Six years of a traveller's life in Western Africa. *v.*1, *p.*120 ; *v.*2, *pp.*220–25, 344. Hurst. 1861. *i.*
Descr. & illust. of Cazembe & Mossamedes instr.

BASTIAN, ADOLF. Die deutsche Expedition an der Loangoküste. *v.*1, *pp.*46, 161–63. Jena : Costenoble. 1874.
Many Ambundu instr. descr.

MONTEIRO, JOACHIM JOHN. Angola & the River Congo. *v.*2, *pp.*138–42. Macmillan. 1875.
Instr. descr. : notation of " Kroomen of R. Zaire " attempted.

SOYAUX, HERMAN. Die Kunst beim Neger [Illustrirte Deut. Monatshefte, 615–22 : 1877] *i.*
Deals with music of ' Lower Guinea ', giving ill. of instr. & notation of 9 tunes.

„ Aus West Africa. *v.*2, *pp.*174–79. Leip. : Brockhaus. 1879.
Good descr. of instr. & notation of three songs.

LUX, A. E. Von Loando nach Kimbunda. *pp.*120–22. Wien : Hölzel. 1880. *i.*
Descr. & illust. of several instr. : see also vocabulary at end of book, for vernacular names.

SERPA PINTO, ALEXANDRE de. How I crossed Africa. *v.*1, *pp.*191, 332. Sampson, Low. 1881.
Descr. Benguella " ramkie " & other instr.

CAPELLO, HERMENEGILDO AUGUSTO de BRITO & IVENS, ROBERT. From Benguella to Yacca. *v.*1, *pp.*138–39. Sampson, Low. 1882.
Attempted notation of Quiteque air given.

DIAS de CARVALHO, HENRIQUE AUGUSTO. Ethnographia e historia dos povos da Lunda. *pp.*364–79. Lisboa : Imprensa Nacional. 1890. *i.*
Good detailed descr. & range of xylophone, string & wind instr.

SEIDEL, AUGUST. Das Geistesleben der afrikanischen Negervölker. *p.*158. Berl. : Schall. 1896.
Includes notation of an Ambundu air.

BASTOS, AUGUSTO. Traços geraes sobre a ethnographia do districto de Benguella [Bol. Soc. Geog. Lisboa, 26 : 176, 197–200 : 1908]
„ *Ditto : separately. pp.*173–78. Famalicão. 1911.
Descr. many instr. & dances.

DINIZ, FERREIRA. Populações indigenas de Angola. *pp.*18, 43, 78, 135–36, 175–76, 217, 233, 242, 265, 328, 354–56, 388, 424, 441, 550. Coimbra : Imprensa da Universidade. 1918.
Brief incidental notes on music & instr. of many tribes.

ANON. An African dulcitone : the Marimba, played in the Ambaca region of Angola [Field, *p.*878, June 24, 1922]

STATHAM, JOHN CHARLES BARRON. Through Angola : a coming colony. *pp.*221–22. Blackwood. 1922.
Brief notes on instr.

SCHACHTZABEL, ALFRED. Im Hochland von Angola. *pp.*62, 104, 111 & Taf.21. Dresden : Deut. Buchwerkstätten. 1923. *i.*
> *Incidental mention of boatsong & instr.*

BLEEK, DOROTHEA F. Buschmänner von Angola [Archiv f. Anthrop., 21 : 53 : 1927]
> *Bushman instr. briefly descr.*

„ Bushmen of Central Angola [Bantu Stud., 3 : 119–21 : 1929] *i.*
> *Contains notation of dance & bow songs, with comments thereon.*

JASPERT, FRITZ & JASPERT, WILLEM. Die Völkerstämme Mittel-Angolas [Veröff. Städt. Völkermus. Frankfurt-a-M., 5] *pp.*104, 134–39. Frankfurt-a-M. 1930. *i.*
> *Informative notes on instr. & singing, with notation of two songs.*

MONARD, A. Note sur les collections ethnographiques de la Mission Scientifique Suisse en Angola [Soc. Neuchât. Géog., 39 : 104–16 : 1930] *i.*
> *Detailed descr. of instr. & manner of playing.*

„ Voyage de la Mission Scientifique Suisse en Angola, 1928–29. [Soc. Neuchât. Géog., 39 : 43–44 : 1930] i.
> *Descr. dance rhythms, gives notation of dance song & good illust. of sansa being played.*

BAUMANN, HERMANN. Die Mannbarkeitsfeiern bei den Tšokwe [Baessler Archiv, Leip., 15 : 47 : 1932]
> *Incidental mention of instr. accompanying ceremonial dances.*

HAMBLY, WILFRID DYSON. Occupational ritual, belief & custom among the Ovimbundu [Amer. Anthrop., 36 : 167 : 1934] *i.*
> *Short note on musicians : see plate 4, illust. of drum & flute players.*

„ The Ovimbundu of Angola [Field Mus. Nat. Hist., Anthrop. Ser., 21 : 216–26 : 1934] Chicago. *i.*
> *Good detailed descr. of instr., drum-rhythms, songs, dance & game music, with notation of several melodies transcribed from phonog. recordings by George Herzog.*

BAUMANN, HERMANN. Lunda. *p.*218 *et seq.* Berl. : Lankwitz. 1935. *m. & i.*
> *Descr. & illust. instr.*

27—SOUTH WEST AFRICA

MORITZ, EDUARD. Die ältesten Reiseberichte über Deutsch-Sudwest-afrika : i., H. J. Wikar, 1778 [Mitt. Schutz., 31 : 73, 87 : 1918]
> *Reed & other dances descr.*

ALEXANDER, *Sir* JAMES EDWARD. Expedition of discovery into the interior of Africa. *v.*1, *pp.*233–34 ; *v.*2, *pp.*162, 182–83. Colburn. 1838.
> *Descr. of Namaqua reed & pot dances.*

„ Report of an expedition of discovery, through the countries of the Great Namáquas, Boschmans & the Hill Dámaras, in South Africa [Jour. R. Geog. Soc., 8 : 19–20 : 1838]
> *Short descr. of Damara reed & pot dance.*

SHAW, BARNABAS. Memorials of S. Afr. *pp.*43–44, 74. Mason. 1840.
Notes on instr. of Namaquas, & Damara reed-dancing.

GALTON, FRANCIS. Narrative of an explorer in tropical S. Africa.
*p.*192. Murray. 1853.
Brief note on guitar, musical bow & singing of Damara.

ANDERSSON, CHARLES JOHN. Lake Ngami. *pp.*230–31. Hurst. 1856.
Musical bow & other instr. of Damaras descr.

BAINES, THOMAS. Explorations in S.W. Africa. *pp.*384–85. Longmans.
1864.
Mention of Damara dance & rattles.

HAHN, THEOPHILUS. Die Nama Hottentoten [Globus, Braunschweig,
12 : 278, 335 : 1867]
Brief notes on Nama singing, goura & other instr.

,, Die Buschmänner [Globus, Braunschweig, 18 : 121–22 : 1870]
*Descr. dancing, singing, drum & goura with notation of melody
from Burchell.*

RIDSDALE, BENJAMIN. Scenes & adventures in Great Namaqualand.
*pp.*94–95. Woolmer. 1883.
Namaqua guitar, goura & drum described.

SCHINZ, HANS. Deutsch-Sudwest Afrika. *pp.*31–32, 95–96. Oldenburg :
Schwartz. 1891.
Hottentot reed dances descr. : note on goura.

GENTZ, P. Beiträge zur Kenntnis der südwestafrikanischen Völker-
schaften [Globus, Braunschweig, 83 : 301 : 1903 ; & 84 : 156–57 :
1903 : & 85 : 82 : 1904] *i.*
*Descr. Herero & Bushman musical bow & other instr., & dances,
with notation of one melody.*

HEILBORN, ADOLF. Die Musik der Naturvölker unserer Kolonien
[Deut. Kol. Zeit., 21 : 347–48´ : 1904]
Contains notation of Bushman songs.

IRLE, I. Die Herero. *p.*125. Gütersloh : Bertelsmann. 1906.
Short account of dances, musical bow & flute.

WERNER, H. Anthropologische, ethnologische, und ethnographische
Beobachtungen über die Heikum- und Kungbuschleute [Zeit. f.
Ethnol., 38 : 251–52 : 1906]
*Notes on songs & dances of the Heikum, with notation of two
melodies.*

SCHULTZE, LEONHARD. Aus Namaland und Kalahari. *pp.*374–83,
644–45. Jena : Fischer. 1907.
*On Hottentot musical bow & reed dance songs, with notation of
several melodies.*

FISCHER, HANS. Musik und Tanz bei den Eingeborenen in Südwest-
afrika [Musik. Wochenbl., 40 : 354–56, 371–73 : 1909]

,, *Ditto* [Allg. Musik. Zeit., 37 : 418–21 : 1910]
*On musical instr. of Hereros & Bastards, with notation of several
reed dance tunes & Bastard song.*

KAUFMANN, HANS. Die Auin [Mitt. Schutz., 23 : 150–51 : 1910]
Brief note on instr.

72

TÖNJES, HERMANN. Ovamboland. pp.81–83. Berl. : Warneck. 1911. *i.*
  Short account of instr. & singing.
FISCHER, EUGEN. Die Rehobother Bastards. pp.276–78. Jena :
  Fischer. 1913.
  Notes on music accompanying dances.
FRANÇOIS, HUGO von. Nama und Damara. pp.228–30. Magdeburg :
  Baensch. [? 1914]
  Discussion of music : notation (" arranged ") of several tunes.
VEDDER, H. Die Bergdama [Abh. Hamburger Univ., Reihe B., v.7]
  v.1, pp.92–95. Hamburg. 1923.
  Descr. of dances & accompanying music.
LEBZELTER, VIKTOR. Eingeborenen in Südwest- und Südafrika.
  pp.41, 119, 207–08, 284. Leip. : Hiersemann. 1934.
  Notes on !Kung & Ovambo drums & other instr. : see also index :
  Trompeten.
DRURY, J. Preliminary report on the anthropological researches carried
  out by Mr. Drury of the S. African Museum in S.W. Africa [Ann.
  S. Afr. Mus., 24/2 : 101–03 & plate 21 : 1935] *i.*
  Descr. reed & other dances of Sandfontein Bushmen with illust.
  showing manner of playing of " rhumkie."

28—RHODESIA, NORTH AND SOUTH

LIVINGSTONE, DAVID & LIVINGSTONE, CHARLES. Narrative of an
  expedition to the Zambesi. pp.254–55. N.Y. : Harper. 1866. *i.*
  Mention of Batoka instr. : see illust. on pp.98, 105, 255.
THOMAS, THOMAS MORGAN. Eleven years in Central Afr. pp.206–07.
  Snow. [1872]
  Several Matabele instr. descr.
MAUCH, CARL. Reisen im Inneren von Sudafrika, 1865–72 [Petermanns
  Erganz., 37 : 43 : 1874]
  Short notes on instr. & singing of the Makalaka.
HOLUB, EMIL. Kulturskizze des Marutse-Mambunda-Reiches. pp.57–
  64, 135–45. Wien : K. K. Geog. Gesell. 1879. *i.*
  Many instr. descr. & illust. (figs. 65–77) : notes on singing and
  dancing.
  „ Sieben Jahre in Süd Afrika. v.2, pp.148–49, 162, 198–200, 294–95.
  Wien : Hölder. 1881.
  „ Seven years in South Africa. v.2, pp.136, 168–72, 223, 228–29,
  259, 264. Sampson, Low. 1881.
  Notes on Barotse bands, instr. & singing.
SERPA PINTO, ALEXANDRE de. How I crossed Africa. v.2, pp.26–28.
  Sampson, Low. 1881.
  Descr. Barotse royal band.
SPILLMANN, JOSEPH. Vom Cap zum Sambesi. p.221. Freiburg i. B. :
  Herder. 1882.
  Descr. Matabele dance with notation of air.

HOLUB, EMIL.   Von der Capstadt ins Land der Maschukulumbe.   *v.*2,
*p.*83.   Wien : Hölder.   1890.
  A Batoka drum descr.
BENT, JAMES THEODORE.   Ruined cities of Mashonaland.   *pp.*75–82.
Longmans.   1893.   *i.*
  Several notes on Makalanga sansa, "jew's harp" & other instr.
BERTRAND, ALFRED.   Au pays des Ba-Rotse.   *pp.*148–49.   Paris.
Hachette.   1898.   *i.*
  *Notes on band of Chief Lewanika.   See illust., pp.*151, 161.
BÉGUIN, EUGENE.   Les Ma-Rotse.   *pp.*144–45.   Lausanne : Benda.   1903.
  Brief descr. of xylo, sansa & drums.
MELLAND, FRANK HULME.   Notes on the ethnography of the Awemba
[Jour. Afr. Soc., 4 : 342–43 : 1905]
  Gives details of drums, stringed instr. & sansa.
PASSARGE, SIEGRIED.   Die Mambukuschu [Globus, Braunschweig,
87 : 296 : 1905] *i.*
  Brief mention & illust. of open-ended drum.
RICHARTZ, F. J.   Habits & customs of the Mashonas [Zambesi Mission
Record, 1 : 551–53 : 1905] *i.*
  Descr. musical bow, drums, rattles & dances.
RICHTER, MARTIN.   Kultur und Reich der Marotse.   *pp.*165–76.   Leip. :
Voigtländer.   1908.
  Discussion on songs, instr. & dances.
GOULDSBURY, CULLEN & SHEANE, HUBERT.   The great plateau of
Northern Rhodesia.   *pp.*263–69.   Arnold.   1911.
  *General remarks on instr. & singing of Awemba with notation of
  several songs.*
VON ROSEN, ERIC.   Träskfolket Svenska Rhodesia-Kongo-Expedi-
tionens etnografiska Forskningsresultat.   *pp.*257–73, 286, 341–51,
369–70, 416–17.   Stockholm.   1916.   *i.*
  *Detailed notes on instr., with map showing their distribution, of
  Babisa, Bushmen & Valenge.*
SMITH, EDWIN W. & DALE, ANDREW MURRAY.   The Ila-speaking
peoples of Northern Rhodesia.   *v.*2, pp.262–69.   Macmillan.   1920.   *i.*
  *Good notes on instr., drums & drumming, with illust. of drums &
  xylos.*
TORREND, JULIUS.   Specimens of Bantu folk-lore from Northern
Rhodesia.   187*pp.*   Kegan Paul.   1921.
  Contains notation of several melodies from phonog. recordings.
STIRKE, D. E. C.   Barotseland.   *pp.*85–92.   Bale.   1922.
  Descr. notes on dances, songs & instr.
MELLAND, FRANK HULME.   In witchbound Africa.   *pp.*282–88.   Seeley,
Service.   1923.   *i.*
  *General remarks on dancing & drumming, with notation of several
  songs.*
SCHEBESTA, PAUL.   Zur ethnographie der Asena am unteren Sambesi
[Bibl. Afr., 2 : 207–08 : 1926]
  Brief enumeration of instr.

TAYLOR, GUY A. Some Mashona songs & dances [Nada, Bulawayo, 3 : 38–42 : 1926]

> Notation of six songs transcribed by J. V. Davidovics, & comment thereon.

BURNIER, THÉOPHILE. Chants zambéziens. 31pp. Paris : Soc. des Miss. Evang. 1927. i.

> Useful discussion on Barotse songs & dances, with notation of 28 melodies.

TAYLOR, M. Did Pharaoh Necho's minstrels visit South Africa ? [Illust. Lond. News, 171 : 1058–59 : 1927] i.

> Descr. rock paintings of musicians discovered in S. Rhodesia.

JALLA, LOUIS. Sur les rives du Zambèze : notes ethnographiques. pp.93–101. Paris : Soc. des Miss. Evang. 1928. i.

> Detailed notes on Barotse instr. & dancing.

TRACEY, HUGH T. Some observations on native music of Southern Rhodesia [Nada, Bulawayo, 7 : 96–103 : 1929]

> Discussion of Makalanga songs, with notation of five airs.

DOKE, CLEMENT M. The Lambas of Northern Rhodesia. pp.357–68. Harrap. 1931. i.

> Good detailed descr. of native " pianos ", drums, flutes & other instr. well illust.

TRACEY, HUGH T. African folk music [Man, 32 : 118–19 : 1932]

> Brief note on Mashona music.

,, The tuning of musical instruments [Nada, Bulawayo, 13 : 35–44 : 1935] i.

> Detailed descr. of Mashona methods of tuning a sansa.

29—UNION OF SOUTH AFRICA, INCLUDING PROTECTORATES

(a) South Africa generally

FRITSCH, GUSTAV. Die Eingeborenen Südafrikas. pp.20, 132–33, 190–91, 225, 327–28, 427, 439–40. Leip. : Hirt. 1872.

> Notes on music of Zulus, Bushmen & Bechuana.

TORREND, J. A comparative grammar of the S.-Afr. Bantu languages. pp.296–320. Kegan Paul. 1891.

> Gives notation of many folk-song melodies & notes on instr.

ROSE, ALGERNON S. Afr. primitive instr. [Pro. Music. Assn., 1903–04 ; 30 : 91–108 : 1904]

,, A private collection of Afr. instr. and S. Afr. clickers [Zeit. Intern. Musikgesell., 6 : 60–66, 283–86 : 1904–05] i.

BALFOUR, HENRY. The musical instr. of S. Afr. [Rept. Brit. Assn., pp.528–29, 1905]

> Abstract of paper dealing with musical bow & many other instr.

MOLEMA, S. M. The Bantu, past & present. pp.162–63. Edinburgh : Green. 1920.

> General remarks on nature of Bantu scale & instr.

KIRBY, PERCIVAL R. Some problems of primitive harmony & polyphony with special reference to Bantu practice [S. Afr. Jour. Sci., 23 : 951–70 : 1926]
> *An attempt to trace evolution of polyphony & the movement of parts in Bantu music.*

WEBB, MAURICE. Music in S. Afr. [Voorslag, Durban, 1 : 23–26 : 1926]
> *General remarks on possibility of giving a native basis to South African music of the future.*

KIRBY, PERCIVAL R. Primitive & exotic music [S. Afr. Jour. Sci., 25 : 507–14 : 1928]
> *Urges need for research : discusses culture contact, primitive polyphony, & the pentatonic scale.*

„ Study of S. Afr. native music [S. Afr. Rlys. Mag., 2001–06 : 1928] *i.*
> *On relation between speech tone & music, & the nature of Bantu music generally.*

WENDT, THEOPHIL. S. Afr. songs for voice & piano (based on native melodies) 6*v. in* 1. N.Y. : Fischer. [1928]
> *See foreword : gives notation of six airs, unarranged.*

SCHUMANN, C. Volksmusik der Eingeborenen [Die Brücke, 7 : 1, 2–8 : 1929]
> *General remarks on nature of music.*

KIRBY, PERCIVAL R. Study of negro harmony [Music. Quart., 16 : 404–14 : 1930]
> *Informative account of the characteristics of Bantu music & effect of European cultures thereon.*

A., T. Bantu music [S. Afr. Outlook, 61 : 116–17 : 1931]
> *Discusses possibility of organising a native eisteddfod.*

ANON. Bantu music on the gramophone [S. Afr. Outlook, 61 : 78 : 1931]
> *Brief account of commercial recordings : of little scientific value.*

KIRBY, PERCIVAL R. The Gora & its Bantu successors [Bantu Stud., 5 : 89–109 : 1931] *i. bibliog.* 2*pp.*
> *Well documented discussion of the gora & kindred instr., with good illust.*

„ The study of the music of the native people [Blythswood Review, 8 : 81–82 : 1931]
> *An appeal for scientific study of native instr. now dying out.*

„ Recognition & practical use of harmonics of stretched strings by the Bantu of S. Afr. [Bantu Stud., 6 : 31–46 : 1932]
> *An attempt to gauge influence of use of harmonics on Bantu scales, harmony and polyphony.*

„ Musical origins in the light of the musical practices of Bushman, Hottentot & Bantu [Pro. Music. Assn., 59 : 23–33 : 1933]
> *Good discussion of the relation of speech & song, & between Bantu polyphony & medieval diaphony.*

„ Reed-flute ensembles of S. Afr. [R. Anthrop. Inst., 63 : 313–88 : 1933] *i.*
> *Exhaustive collation of data regarding construction, use & technical detail of reed flutes : well illust. (see plates 18–26)*

SPEIGHT, W. L. The evolution of native music [Sackbut, 14 : 18–20 : 1933]
   An appeal for the encouragement of indigenous music in native education.
KIRBY, PERCIVAL R. The effects of Western civilisation on Bantu music. *In* Western civilisation & the natives of S. Afr., ed. Isaac Schapera. *pp.*131–40. Routledge. 1934.
   Important discussion on European influences on music & instr. & the need for an indigenous school of music to replace present decay.
„ The musical instr. of the native races of S. Afr. 296*pp.* Milford. 1934. *m. & i.*
   Exhaustive study of instr. with many references & illust., glossary of Afr. names, notation, & many excellent illust. See important critique by HORNBOSTEL, E. M. von, *in* Nature, *v.*136, *pp.*3–5, 1935.
SPEIGHT, W. L. Notes on S. Afr. music [Music. Quart., 20 : 344–83 : 1934]
   General disconnected remarks on instr. & musical education.
KIRBY, PERCIVAL R. The principle of stratification as applied to S. Afr. native music [S. Afr. Jour. Sci., 32 : 72–90, 1935] *bibliog. & i.*
   An attempt to show the importance of precision in musicology, illust. from history of S. Afr. instr.
LIEBERMAN, HELENA. The music of the S. Afr. natives [African World, 132 : 162 : 1935]
   Popular short account of rhythms & instr.
DUBE, JOHN L. & DUBE, NOKUTELA. Amagama Abantu awe mishado imiququmbelo, ntando nawe mikekelo no kudhlala. 31*pp.* Phœnix : Oklange. n.d.
   An African national anthem : " God bless Africa ".

(b) *Bushmen and Hottentots*

MORELET, ARTHUR. Journal du voyage de Vasco da Gama en 1497. *p.*9. Lyons : Perrin. 1864.
   Descr. Hottentot flute-greeting at the Cape.
SCHAPERA, ISAAC & FARRINGTON, B., *eds.* The early Cape Hottentots [Van Riebeeck Soc. 14] *pp.*35, 76, 77, 149, 213. Cape Town. 1933.
   Descr. by early travellers of Namaqua reed-ensemble, drums, flutes & harmony.
WATERHOUSE, GILBERT. Simon van der Stel's journal of his expedition into Namaqualand, 1685–86. *pp.*46–47, 133–34. Dublin : U.P. 1932.
   Brief references to reed dances : see also notes to plates 99 & 162.
TACHARD, G. Voyage de Siam des Pères Jésuites, envoyez par le Roy aux Indes & à la Chine. *pp.*102–03, 106. Paris : Seneuze. 1686.
   Good descr. of Namaqua flute ensembles & dances.
VALENTYN, FRANÇOIS. Oud en Nieuw Oost Indien. *v.*5, *pt.*2, *p.*105b. Dordrecht : van Braam. 1726.
   Brief descr. of Hottentot goura.

KOLBE, PETER. Reise an das Capo du Bonne Esperance oder das afrikanische Vorgebürge der Guten Hofnung. *pp*.527–31. Nurnberg : Monath. 1719.

„ The present state of the Cape of Good Hope. *pp*.155, 239, 271–81. Innys. 1731. *i.*
   Note on Hottentot instr., including " gom-gom", singing & dancing.

„ Reise zum Vorgebirge der Guten Hoffnung. *pp*.122–24. Leip. : Brockhaus. 1926.
   Abridged edition of the above.

BEUTLER, VAANDRIG AUGUST FREDERIK. Landtocht naar het Kafferland (1752). *In* GODÉE-MOLSBERGEN, E. C. (*ed*). Reizen in Zuid Afrika [Linschoten-Vereeniging Werken, 20] *p*.310. Amsterdam. 1922.
   Hottentot instr. descr.

LA CAILLE, NICHOLAS LOUIS de. Journal historique du voyage fait au Cap de Bonne Espérance. *pp*.192–93. Paris : Guillyn. 1763.
   Detailed description of " Kaffir " mbila.

SPARRMANN, ANDREAS. Voyage to Cape of Good Hope. *v*.1, *pp*.228–30 ; *v*.2, *pp*.28–9, 356. Robinson. 1785.
   Brief observations on goura, drums & singing, with notation of an air.

MENTZEL, O. F. Beschreibung des Vorgebirges der Guten Hoffnung. *v*.2, *pp*.513–14, 516–19. Glogau : Günther. 1787.
   Careful account of reed-flute dances & instr. of Hottentots.

PATERSON, WILLIAM. A narrative of four journeys into the country of the Hottentots of Caffraria. *p*.57. Johnson. 1789.
   Short descr. of reed dance.

WINKELMAN, FRANZ von. Reisaantekeningen (1788–89). *In* GODÉE-MOLSBERGEN, E. C. (*ed*) : Reizen in Zuid Afrika [Linschoten-Vereeniging Werken, 36] *pp*.81–84. Amsterdam. 1932.
   Good descr. of " Kaffir " dances, singing & instr.

LE VAILLANT, FRANÇOIS. Voyage dans l'intérieur de l'Afrique par le Cap de Bonne Espérance dans les années, 1780–85. *v*.2, *pp*.247–49, 343. Paris : Leroy. 1790.

„ Travels from the Cape of Good Hope into the interior parts of Africa. *v*.1, *pp*.429–30 ; *v*.2, *pp*.122–30. Lane. 1790.
   Good descr. of goura, rommelpot & other instr. of Hottentots.

THUNBERG, CARL PETER. Travels in . . . Africa, . . . 1770 & 1779. *v*.1, *pp*.218, 233 ; *v*.2, *pp*.43–44, 78. 1795. *i.*
   Detailed descr. of several instr. ; see plate 1, v.2.

BARROW, *Sir* JOHN. An account of travels into the interior of S. Afr., 1797–98. *v*.1, *pp*.148–49. Cadell. 1801–04.
   Descr. of goura.

BARRINGTON, GEORGE. Account of a voyage to New South Wales. *v*.1, *pp*.189–90, 218, 250–51. Jones. 1803.
   Descr. Hottentot instr., including gabourie & goura.

PERCIVAL, ROBERT. An account of the Cape of Good Hope. *pp*.91–92. Baldwin. 1804.
   Good descr. of gabourie & goura.

ALBERTI, LODEWYK. De Kaffers aan de Zuidkust van Afrika. *pp.*165–66. Amsterdam : Maskaamp. 1810.
„ Description physique et historique des Cafres sur la côte méridionale de l'Afrique. *pp.*165–66. Amsterdam : Maskaamp. 1811.
   Descr. Gonaquois bow instr.
LICHTENSTEIN, MARTIN HEINRICH KARL. Reizen im Südlichen Afrika in den Jahren 1803–06. *v.*1, *pp.*44–45, 150, 247–48 ; *v.*2, *pp.*379–80, 549–50. Berl. : Salfeld. 1811.
„ Travels in Southern Afr. in years 1803–06. *v.*1, *pp.*28, 94, 153–54 ; *v.*2, *pp.*232–33, 337–38. Colburn. 1812–15.
   Good descr. of goura & singing of the Hottentots : notes on Korana music.
BURCHELL, WILLIAM JOHN. Travels in the interior of Southern Afr. *v.*1, *pp.*458, 499–500 ; *v.*2, *pp.*24, 45, 63–67, 287–88. Longmans. 1822. *i.*
   Good descr. of Bushman goura & " violin ", and Hottentot songs & dancing.
THOMPSON, GEORGE. Travels & adventures in Southern Afr. *v.*1, *pp.*339, 422. Colburn. 1827. *i.*
   Note on rattles, ramakie, mbila & Bushman dance.
WEBSTER, WILLIAM HENRY BAILEY. Narrative of a voyage to the S. Atlantic Ocean in 1828–30. *v.*1, *pp.*274–75. Bentley. 1834.
   Note on Hottentot goura & dance.
MOODIE, JOHN WEDDERBURN DUNBAR. Ten years in S. Afr. *v.*1, *pp.*224–29. Bentley. 1835.
   Goura & other instr. descr. : notation of three Hottentot airs given.
ARBOUSSET, J. THOMAS, & DAUMAS, F. Relation d'un voyage d'exploration au nord-est de la Colonie du Cap de Bonne-Espérance. *pp.*54, 487–91. Paris : Bertrand. 1842.
   Descr. Korana pot dance.
MOFFAT, ROBERT. Missionary labours & scenes in S. Afr. *p.*58. Snow. 1842.
   Brief note on goura.
BACKHOUSE, JAMES. Narrative of a visit to the Mauritius & S. Afr. *pp.*445, 463–64, 504. Adams. 1844.
   Mention of Bushman goura & fiddle.
SUTHERLAND, JOHN. Memoir respecting the Kaffers, Hottentots & Bosjemans of S. Afr. *v.*2, *pp.*245, 647–48. Capetown : Pike. 1845.
   Namaqua reed dance described from diary of Pieter Meerhoff & Van der Stel.
BORCHERDS, PETRUS BORCHARDUS. Autobiographical memoir. *pp.*114, 178. Cape Town : Robertson. 1861.
   On Bushman rommelpot, goura & ramakienjo.
HAHN, THEOPHILUS. Tsuni-Goam, the supreme being of Khoi-khoi. *pp.*27–29. 1881.
   Reed songs descr.
THULIÉ, M. Sur les Bochimans [Bul. Soc. Anthrop. Paris, 4 : 404 : 1881]
   Goura descr. in detail.

HELLWALD, FRIEDRICH von. Naturgeschichte des Menschen. *v.*2, *p.*20. Stuttgart : Spemann. [1882]
 Brief note on Bushman drum & dances, with notation of a melody.

METCHNIKOFF, LÉON. Bushmen et Hottentots [Soc. Neuchât. Géog., 5 : 76 : 1889–90]
 Enumerates Bushman instr.

LLOYD, LUCY C. A short account of further Bushman material collected by L.C.L. *pp.*17–18. Nutt. 1899.
 Brief references to drums, rattles & !gom !gom.

BALFOUR, HENRY. The " Goura ", a stringed-wind musical instr. of the Bushmen Hottentots [R. Anthrop. Inst., 32 : 156–78 : 1902] *i.*
 A comparison of the goura & musical bow.

KIDD, DUDLEY. Essential Kaffir. *pp.*332–35. Black. 1904. *i.*
 General notes on Damara bows, mbilas & other instr.

STOW, GEORGE W. The native races of S. Afr. *pp.*102–16, 253, 262, 547. Swan, Sonnenschein. 1905.
 Notes on instr. of Bushmen, Namaquas & Hereros, & reed-flute dances, with notation of several airs.

PASSARGE, SIEGFRIED. Buschmänner der Kalahari. *pp.*95–98. Berl. : Reimer. 1907.
 Notes on songs & instr. of Bushmen, including goura.

DUNN, EDWARD JOHN. Ethnological collections made in S. Afr. 44*pp.* Kew, Victoria. 1908.
 Descr. goura & several other instr.

BLEEK, E. & BLEEK, DOROTHEA F. [Note on songs & instr.] *In* TONGUE, M. H. : Bushman paintings. *pp.*36–37. Oxf. : U. P. 1909.

TONGUE, M. HELEN. Bushman paintings. *p.*39 & plates 14, 15, 36. Oxf. : U. P. 1909. *i.*
 Interesting illust. showing instr. in use.

BARNARD, *Lady* ANNE. S. Afr. a century ago. *pp.*259–60. Smith, Elder. 1910.
 Brief mention of Hottentot goura.

BLEEK, WILHELM HEINRICH IMMANUEL & LLOYD, LUCY C. Specimens of Bushman folklore. Allen. *pp.*351–57. *i.*
 Notes on drums & dancing rattles.

GRETSCHEL, E. Die Buschmannsammlung Hannemann [Jahrb. Städt. Mus. Völk. Leip., 5 : 110–12 : 1911–12] *i.*
 Bushman dance instr. descr. & illust.

DORNAN, SAMUEL S. Tati Bushmen (Masarwas) & their language [R. Anthrop. Inst., 47 : 44, 53–55 : 1917]
 Notes on rattles, dances & songs, with notation (" arranged ") of hunting song.

BLEEK, DOROTHEA F. The Naron. *pp.*21–22, 25. Camb. : U. P. 1928.
 General remarks on Bushman monochord & other instr., singing & dancing.

SCHAPERA, ISAAC. The Khoisan peoples of S. Afr. *pp.*206–07, 400–05. Routledge. 1930.
 On goura, reed-dances & musical pantomime of Bushmen & Hottentots.

STOW, GEORGE W. *In* BLEEK, D. F. : Rock paintings in S. Afr. **Plate**
72. Methuen. 1930.
Illust. of Bushman bow.

DUNN, EDWARD JOHN. The Bushman. *pp.*40–41. Griffin. 1931.
Brief note on instr.

KIRBY, PERCIVAL R. The mystery of the grand gom gom [S. **Afr.**
Jour. Sci., 28 : 521–25 : 1931] *i.*
Informative discussion of instr., first mentioned by Kolbe.

„ Musical origins in the light of the musical practices of Bushman,
Hottentot & Bantu [Pro. Music. Assn., 59 : 23–33 : 1933]
*Good discussion of the relation of speech & song, & between Bantu
polyphony & medieval diaphony.*

„ A further note on the goura & its Bantu successors [Bantu Stud.,
9 : 53–56 : 1935] *i.*
*A closer examination of Burchell's evidence, discussing manner of
playing goura.*

„ A study of Bushman music [Bantu Stud., 10 : 205–52 : 1936]
bibliog. 3pp.
*Critical examination of Bushman songs noted by Lucy C. Lloyd &
transcribed by C. Weisbecker ; with correlation of earlier evidence &
notation of 21 songs.*

(c) *Zulu-Xosa*

DOS SANTOS, JOAÑO. Ethiopia Oriental (1609). *In* THEAL, G. M. :
Records of S. E. Afr. *v.*7, *pp.*202–03, 354. Swan, Sonnenschein.
1901.
Good observations on Zulu mbila, horns & drums.

CAMPBELL, JOHN. Travels in S. Africa. *pp.*433, 518–19. Black.
1815. *i.*
Remarks on dancing & instr. See also plate V.

ROSE, COWPER. Four years in Southern Afr. *pp.*141, 146. Colburn.
1829.
" Kaffir " oxhide & shield-drums briefly described.

KAY, STEPHEN. Travel & researches in Caffraria. *p.*373. Mason. 1833.
Mention of " Kaffir " singing & " fugues ".

GARDINER, ALLEN FRANCIS. Narrative of a journey to the Zoolu
country. *pp.*56–59, 104–05. Crofts. 1836. *i.*
Short account of rattles & other Zulu instr. : see plate I.

ANGAS, GEORGE FRENCH. The Kaffirs illustrated. Hogarth. 1849.
See plates 17, 19 & 25 for illust. of Zulu reedpipe, rattles & bow.

SHOOTER, JOSEPH. The Kaffirs of Natal & the Zulu country. *pp.* 234–38.
Stanford. 1857.
*On Zulu dances & songs : notation of four airs & notes on
instr.*

GROUT, LEWIS. Zululand. *pp.*194 *et seq.* Philadelphia : Presbyterian
Publications Cttee. 1860.
Brief notes on Zulu instr. & songs.

81

HOLDEN, WILLIAM CLIFFORD. The past & future of the Kaffir races. *pp.*265–72. Published by author. [1866] *i.*
General remarks on songs & singing: see illust. of "gubu" (*figure* 17).

CHAPMAN, JAMES. Travels in the interior of S. Afr. *v.*1, *pp.*91–92, 405. Bell & Dady. 1868.
Describes Bushman & Namaqua dances.

CALLAWAY, HENRY. Religious system of the Amazulu [Publ. of Folk Lore Soc., 15] *pp.*409–13. Trübner. 1870.
Notes on Zulu songs.

MACKENZIE, JOHN. Ten years north of the Orange River. *p.*328. Edinburgh : Edmonston. 1871. *i.*
Note on goura.

DAVIS, WILLIAM J. Kaffir-English dictionary. 332*pp.* Wesleyan Mission House. 1872.
See under names of native instr.

SCULLY, WILLIAM CHARLES & SCULLY, NORA. Kaffir music [Pall Mall Mag., 12 : 179 : 1897]
Brief general account.

SCULLY, WILLIAM CHARLES. Kaffir music. *In his :* By veldt & kopje. *pp.*285–301. Fisher Unwin. 1907.
Discussion on songs, with notation of several airs.

MAYR, FRANZ. Short study on Zulu music [Ann. Natal Mus., 1/3 : 241–55 : 1908]
Good short account of music & instr., with notation.

AITCHISON, S. G. GILKES. Native social life. *pp.*26–29. Durban : Jones. 1917.
Describing Zulu singing & instr.

CURTIS, NATALIE BURLIN. Songs & tales from the Dark Continent. *pp.*133–49. N. Y. : Schirmer. 1920.
Zulu songs descr. & illust. by notation.

KIRBY, PERCIVAL R. Old time chants of Mpumuza chiefs [Bantu Stud., 2 : 23–34 : 1923]
Detailed analysis & discussion of songs with notation from phonog. recordings.

SAMUELSON, ROBERT CHARLES AZARIAH. King Cetewayo Zulu Diction-ary. 995*pp.* Durban : Commercial Printing Co. 1923.
See vernacular names of instr.

SAMUELSON, L. H. Zululand : its traditions, legends, customs & folklore. *pp.*144–46. Marianhill : Miss. Press. [1928]
Short notes on ritual instr., with notation of " national anthem ".

SAMUELSON, ROBERT CHARLES AZARIAH. Long, long ago. *pp.*319–21, 386–87. Durban : Knox Printing Co. 1929.
Notes on Zulu dances, songs & instr.

CALUZA, REUBEN TOLAKELE. African music [S. Workman, 60 : 152–55 : 1931]
General remarks on nature of Zulu music.

Cook, Peter Alan Wilson. Social organisation & ceremonial institutions of the Bomvana. *pp.*62–71. Cape Town : Juta. [1931]
Note on initiation drum & notation of one ritual melody.

Plant, R. W. Notes on native musical instr. [Blythswood Review, 8 (Supplt.) : 97 : 1931)
Notes on six Xosa instr.

Scully, Nora. Native tunes heard & collected in Basutoland [Bantu Stud., 5 : 247–52 : 1931]
Contains notation of 17 Basuto & Zulu tunes & discussion thereon.

Kirby, Percival R. The drums of the Zulu [S.Afr. Jour. Sci., 29 : 655–59 : 1932] *i.*
Detailed descr. of construction & manner of playing of many drums.

Werner, Alice. Myths & legends of the Bantu. *pp.*240, 284. Harrap. 1933. *i.*
Good illust. of " Kaffir piano " & umqangala.

Caluza, Reuben Tolakele. Three Zulu songs. *In* Negro anthology, ed. Nancy Cunard. *pp.*415–16. Wishart. 1934.
Gives notation of three songs from phonog. recordings.

Krige, Eileen Jensen. The social system of the Zulus. *pp.*77, 336–44. Longmans. 1936.
Contains informative chapter on music, dancing & song.

(d) Sotho-Chuana

Burchell, William John. Travels in the interior of Southern Africa. *v.*2, *pp.*410–13, 437–38, 578, 598–99. Longmans. 1822. *i.*
Bechuana reed dance, singing & whistles, descr. with notation of Bechuana songs.

Campbell, John. Travels in S. Afr. *v.*1, *pp.*84–85. Westley. 1822.
Brief descr. of Bechuana reed dance.

Arbousset, J. T. & Daumas, F. Relation d'un voyage d'exploration au nord-est de la Colonie du Cap de Bonne-Espérance. *pp.*400, 490–91. Paris : Bertrand. 1842.
Bechuana rattles & xylo descr.

Zerwick, *** [Note on Bechuana reed dance] [Berliner Missionsberichte, 11 : 180–81 : 1855]

Livingstone, David. Missionary travels & researches in S. Afr. *p.*225. Murray. 1857. *i.*
Illust. of " Bechuana " reed dance.

Casalis, Eugène. Les Bassoutos. *pp.*155–58, 360–62. Paris : Meyrueis. 1859.

,, The Basutos. *pp.*148–50, 344–47. Nisbet. 1861.
Notes on drums, rattles, singing & songs : notation of several folksongs.

Chapman, James. Travels in the interior of S. Afr. *v.*1, *pp.*271–72. Bell & Dady. 1868.
Bechuana reeds & musical bow descr.

WANGEMANN, HERMANN THEODOR. Ein zweites Reisejahr in Süd-Afrika. *pp*.140, 158, 161–62, 167. Berl. : Verlag des Missionhauses. 1886.
 Descr. Venda flutes, bows, mbilas & other instr.

ANDERSON, ANDREW ARTHUR. Twenty-one years in a wagon in the gold regions of Africa. *v*.1, *pp*.106, 140–41, 176. Chapman & Hall. 1887.
 Bechuana reed band briefly descr.

WIDDICOMBE, JOHN. Fourteen years in Basutoland. *pp*.58–59: Church Printing Co. 1891.
 Notes on drum, goura, & guitar.

MARTIN, MINNIE. Basutoland : its legends & customs. *pp*.48–49. Nichols. 1903.
 Brief descr. of " moropa" drum.

MABILLE, H. E. The Basutos of Basutoland [Jour. Afr. Soc., 5 : 241–42 : 1905–06]
 General remarks on instr. & musical talent of Basutos.

PASSARGE, SIEGFRIED. Das Okawangosumpfland und seine Bewohner [Zeit. f. Ethnol., 37 : 684–85 : 1905]
 Several instr. briefly descr.

 „ Südafrika. *pp*.239–41. Leip. : Quelle. 1908. *m.*
 References to various Basuto instr., with distribution map (from Ankerman : Die afrikanischen Musikinstrumenten, 1901).

WESSMANN, R. The Bawenda of the Spelonken, Transvaal. *p*.30. African World. 1908.
 Describes a mbila.

NORTON, WILLIAM ALFRED. Sesuto songs & music [S. Afr. Jour. Sci., 6 : 314–16 : 1909]

 „ African native melodies [S. Afr. Assn. Adv. Sci., 12 : 619–28 : 1916]
 Discussion on pentatonic scale & rhythm of Basuto songs : these two articles are identical, except that the latter contains notation in sol-fa.

ROBERTS, NOEL. Bantu methods of divination [S. Afr. Jour. Sci., 13 : 406–08 : 1916]
 Descr. ritual drums.

ENDEMANN, CHRISTIAN. Sotholieder [Mitt. Sem. Orient. Sprach. Afr. Stud., 31 : 14–62 : 1928]
 Gives notation of seventeen tunes & comment thereon.

LESTRADE, G. P. The Bavenda. *p*.21 & plates 16 & 17. Camb. : U. P. 1928. *i.*
 Brief note on instr. & good illust. of horns, etc.

JUNOD, HENRI PHILIPPE. The Mbila or native piano of the T/opi tribe [Bantu Stud., 3 : 275–85, 1929] *i.*
 Good detailed descr. of manufacture & method of playing mbilas.

SCULLY, NORA. Native tunes heard & collected in Basutoland [Bantu Stud., 5 : 247–52 : 1931]
 Contains notation of 17 Basuto & Zulu tunes & discussion thereon.

STAYT, HUGH ARTHUR. The Bavenda [Intern. Inst. Afr. Langs. & Cults.]
   pp.53–54, 210, 227, 316–38. Oxf. : U. P. 1931. *i*.
      *Notes on several instr. & reed-dances, with notation of folk-songs :
      construction & manner of playing of drums descr.*
VAN HOEPEN, A. E. Op soek na 'n Bawenda-Trommel [Die Huis-
   genoot, 33, 77 : 1931]
KIRBY, PERCIVAL R. The music & musical instr. of the Korana [Bantu
   Stud., 6 : 183–203 : 1932] *i*.
      Descr. results of extensive field work : well illust.
VAN WARMELO, N. J. Contributions towards Venda history, religion
   & tribal ritual [Union of S. Afr., Dept. of Native Affairs, Ethnol.
   Publ., v.3] *pp*.192–96. Pretoria : Government Printer. 1932.
      *Descr. reed flute ensembles & contains many incidental references
      to ritual music & instr.*

30—MADAGASCAR

ELLIS, WILLIAM. History of Madagascar. *v*.1, *pp*.272–74. Fisher. 1858.
      Brief notes on instr.
SIBREE, JAMES. Madagascar & its people. *pp*.234–35. Religious
   Tract Soc. [1870]
      Short descr. of singing & instr.
SADOUL, *** Madagascar [Bul. Soc. Anthrop. Paris, 7 : 586–87 : 1896]
      Brief note on songs.
COLIN, E. Mélodies malgaches, recueillies et harmonisées. 68*pp*.
   Antananarivo : Impr. Miss. Catholique. 1899.
GAUTIER, JUDITH. Les chants de Madagascar. *In* Les musiques
   bizarres à l'Exposition de 1900. 28*pp*. Paris : Ollendorff. 1900.
      *Contains notation (" arranged by Benedictus ") of several airs : of
      little scientific value.*
TIERSOT, JULIEN. La musique à Madagascar [Ménestrel, Paris, 35–42 :
   273–74, 281–82, 289–90, 297–99, 305–07, 313–14, 321–33, 328–30 :
   1902]
      *General remarks on instr., singing & songs, with notation from
      Colin : a secondary source.*
SICHEL, A. La musique des Malgaches [Rev. Music., 6 : 389–91,
   448–52 : 1906] *i*.
      Instr. descr. in some detail.
LEBLOND, MARIUS-ARY. La grande île de Madagascar. *pp*.163–80.
   Paris : Delagrave. 1907.
      Rhetorical discussion of Malagasy music.
GRANDIDIER, ALFRED & GRANDIDIER, GUILLAUME. Histoire physique,
   naturelle et politique de Madagascar. *v*.4, *pp*.66–67. Paris : Soc.
   d'Editions Géog., Marit. et Col. 1908–14.
      Brief mention of instr. & singing.
LEBLOND, MARIUS-ARY. Lettre sur la musique malgache [S.I.M.,
   Paris, 4 : 877–87 : 1908]
      General survey of Malagasy music.

HORNBOSTEL, ERICH M. von. Phonographierte Melodien aus Madagaskar und Indonesien. *In* Forschungsreise S.M.S. Planet, 1906–7. *v.5, pp.139–52 & append. pp.1–12.* Berl. : Sigismund. 1909.
> *Detailed analysis of Malagasy melodies from phonog. recordings.*

CAMBOUÉ, P. P. Jeux des enfants malgaches [Anthropos, Wien, 6 : 674 *et seq. :* 1911]
> *Gives notation of children's game-songs.*

KAUDERN, WALTER. På Madagascar. *pp.124–28.* Stockholm : Albert Bonniers Förlag. 1913. *i.*
> *Descr. several instr.*

SICHEL, A. Histoire de la musique des Malgaches. *In* Encyclopédie de la musique et dictionnaire du Conservatoire, ed. Lavignac. *v.5, pt.1, pp.3226–33.* Paris. 1922.
> *Survey of Malagasy music.*

TIERSOT, JULIEN. La musique chez les nègres d'Afrique. *In* Encyclopédie de la musique et dictionnaire du Conservatoire, ed. Lavignac. *v.5, pt.1, pp.3214–3223.* Paris. 1922. *i.*
> *Valiha described, with notation of airs.*

PETIT, GEORGES. Collection ethnographique provenant de Madagascar [L'Anthrop., 33 : 364 : 1923]
> *Instr. called " farai " described.*

RABEARIVELO, J. J. Notes sur la musique malgache [Revue d'Afrique, Paris, 48 : 29–31 : 1931]

LINTON, RALPH. The Tanala [Field Mus. Nat. Hist., Anthrop. Ser., 22 : 264–71 : 1933] *i.*
> *Good descr. & illust. of instr.*

RASON, MARIE-ROBERT. Etude sur la musique malgache [Rev. Madag., 1 : 41–91 : 1933] *i.*
> *Useful historical account, with good descr. & illust. of many instr.*

RUSILLON, H. Un petit continent : Madagascar. *pp.201–03.* Paris : Soc. des Miss. Evang. 1933.
> *Brief notes on music.*

IV.—AFRICAN SURVIVALS IN THE NEW WORLD

1—NEGRO MUSIC IN THE UNITED STATES

CRESSWELL, NICHOLAS. Journal of Nicholas Cresswell, 1774-1777. *pp.18–19.* N.Y. : Lincoln MacVeagh. 1924.
> *The earliest record of Negro folksong : descr. of banjo & Negro music.*

ASHE, THOMAS. Travels in America in 1806. *v.1, p.233.* Phillips. 1808.
> *Descr. Negro band in Virginia.*

FAUX, W. Memorable days in America. *pp.78, 420.* Simpkin & Marshall. 1823.
> *Descr. slave-songs at Charleston.*

GILMAN, CAROLINA. Recollections of a Southern matron. *pp.*76, 78–79, 92, 122. N.Y. : Harper. 1838.
   A lively account of a Negro band.
KEMBLE, FRANCES ANNE. Journal of a residence on a Georgian plantation in 1838–39. *pp.*159–60, 277–79. Longmans. 1863.
   Descr. Negro boat songs.
BARTON, WILLIAM ELEAZAR. Old plantation hymns. 45*pp.* Boston : Lamson. 1899.
   Contains historical & descriptive notes.
MURPHY, JEANNETTE ROBINSON. Survival of African music in America [Popular Science Monthly, N.Y., 55 : 660–72 : 1899]
   Attempts to show that many Afr. characteristics survive : illust. by notation.
BURLEIGH, HARRY T. Plantation melodies, old & new. 18*pp.* N.Y. : Schirmer. 1901.
FERRERO, FELICE. La musica dei negri americani [Riv. Music. Ital., 13 : 391–436 : 1906]
   A general account, with notation ; of little critical value.
KREHBIEL, HENRY EDWARD. Afro-American folksongs. xii.176*pp.* N.Y. : Schirmer. [1914]
   Informative discussion of Afr. elements in American Negro folksong ; with notation.
PORTER, GRACE CLEVELAND. Negro folk singing & games. xix.35*pp.* Curwen. 1914.
   Contains text & melodies.
GOLDSTEIN, WALTER. The natural harmonic & rhythmic sense of the Negro. [Pro. Music Teachers' Nat. Assn., 29–39 : 1917]
   Good discussion on Negro musical ability.
HARE, MAUD CUNEY. Afro-American folksong contribution [Music. Observ., 15/2 : 13, 21 : 1917]
   Popular summary of data from early travellers.
GAUL, HARVEY B. Negro spirituals [New Music Rev., 17 : 147, 151 : 1917]
   Very general remarks on syncopation, etc.
CURTIS, NATALIE BURLIN. Negro folk songs : Hampton Series. 4*v.* N. Y. 1918–19.
   See short introductions to each volume.
WHITE, NEWMAN IVEY. Racial traits in Negro song [Sewanee Rev., July 1920]
   General observations only.
TALLEY, THOMAS WASHINGTON. Negro folk rhymes, wise & otherwise. *pp.*303–07. N.Y. : Macmillan. 1922.
   Notes on Negro musical instr.
SMITH, JOSEPH HUTCHINSON. Folk songs of the American Negro [Sewanee Rev., April 1924] 21*pp.*
   Survey of origins, from Krehbiel & others.
BALLANTA, NICHOLAS GEORGE JULIUS. Saint Helena Island spirituals. *pp.*v–xviii. N.Y. : Schirmer. 1925.
   Discusses African elements surviving in American Negro music : rhythm, cadence, etc.

LOCKE, ALAIN, *ed.* The new Negro. *pp.*199 *et seq.* N.Y. : Boni. 1925.
General survey of Negro spirituals : see good bibliog. of collections,
*commentaries & arrangements, pp.*434–38.

ODUM, HOWARD W. & JOHNSON, GUY BENTON. The Negro & his songs.
vii., 306*pp.* Chapel Hill : Univ. of N. Carolina Press. 1925.
Discusses text of songs, with incidental references to music.

SCARBOROUGH, DOROTHY. On the trail of Negro folk songs. 289*pp.*
Camb., Mass. : Harvard U. P. 1925.
Good collection of many types of song.

COEUROY, ANDRÉ & SCHAEFFNER, ANDRÉ. Le Jazz. 150*pp.* Paris :
Aveline. 1926. *bibliog.* 4*pp.*
On the supposed evolution of jazz from Afr. Negro music : well
documented.

ENGEL, CARL. Views & reviews [Music. Quart., 12 : 306–14, 1926]
Notes on origins of spirituals, & research on Negro folk music.

HORNBOSTEL, ERICH M. von. American Negro songs [Intern. Rev.
Miss., 15 : 748–53 : 1926]
Good summary of the issues involved, concluding that " the manner
of singing only is African ".

JOHNSON, GUY BENTON. Some recent contributions to the study of
American Negro songs [Social Forces, Chapel Hill, 5 : 788–92 : 1926]

JOHNSON, JAMES WELDON. The book of American Negro spirituals.
187*pp.* Chapman & Hall. 1926.
*See preface, pp.*11–50, *for discussion of Afr. elements in spirituals.*

ODUM, HOWARD W. & JOHNSON, GUY BENTON. Negro workaday songs.
*pp.*241–70. Chapel Hill : Univ. of N. Carolina Press. 1926.
Gives examples of Negro tunes, with notation, & from phono-
*photographic records : see bibliog., pp.*265–70.

SCHAEFFNER, ANDRÉ. Notes sur la musique des Afro-Américains
[Ménestrel, Paris, 88 : 285–87, 297–300, 309–12, 321–23, 329–32,
337–39, 345–47 : 1926]
Summary of data concerning Afr. W. Coast music & early Negro
music in the New World.

DETT, ROBERT NATHANIEL. Religious folksongs of the Negro. 236*pp.*
Hampton : Hampton Institute. 1927.

HORNBOSTEL, ERICH M. von. Ethnologisches zu Jazz [Melos, Berl.,
6 : 510–12 : 1927]
A short estimate of Afr. influences surviving in Negro music.

JOHNSON, GUY BENTON. The Negro & musical talent [S. Workman,
56 : 439 : 1927]
Brief critique of theory of Negro harmonic superiority.

WHITE, NEWMAN IVEY. American Negro folksongs. 501*pp.* *bibliog.*
17*pp.* Camb. : Harvard U. P. 1928.
Good discussion on origin & development of Negro songs, with
excellent bibliog.

EMERSON, WILLIAM CANFIELD. Stories & spirituals of the Negro
slaves. 79*pp.* Boston : Badger. 1930.
Contains notation.

HERSKOVITS, MELVILLE JEAN. The Negro in the New World [Amer.
Anthrop., 32 : 145–55 : 1930]
Good general statement of the problems of African survival.
JOHNSON, GUY BENTON. Folk culture on St. Helena Island. *pp.*63–130.
Chapel Hill : Univ. of N. Carolina Press. 1930.
*An important discussion on the development of the spiritual,
emphasising the English-American background.*
KIRBY, PERCIVAL R. Study of Negro harmony [Music. Quart., 16 :
404–14 : 1930]
Compares characteristics of S. Afr. Bantu & American Negro songs.
LAUBENSTEIN, PAUL FRITZ. Race values in Afro-American music
[Music. Quart., 16 : 378–403 : 1930]
*Good discussion of survivals, emphasising the African religious
contribution.*
WARD, WILLIAM ERNEST FRANK. On Negro spirituals & jazz [Teachers'
Jour., G.C., 2/9 : 123–26 : 1930]
An estimate by a music teacher with Afr. experience.
JOHNSON, GUY BENTON. The Negro spiritual : a problem in anthro-
pology [Amer. Anthrop., 33 : 151–71 : 1931]
Careful examination of the problem of origins.
SARGANT, NORMAN & SARGANT, TOM. Negro-American music, or the
origin of jazz [Music. Times, 72 : 653–55, 751–52, 847–48 : 1931]
Popular account of Negro folk song.
TURNER, LUCIEN PRICE. Negro spirituals in the making [Music.
Quart., 17 : 480–85 : 1931]
Describes the process of impromptu spiritual singing.
DAWSON, WARRINGTON. Le caractère spécial de la musique nègre en
Amérique [Jour. Soc. Américanistes, 24 : 273–86 : 1932]
General remarks on spirituals & their preservation.
JACKSON, GEORGE PULLEN. The genesis of the Negro spiritual
[American Mercury, 243–48 : 1932]
*Discussion of origins, emphasising part played by " white
spirituals ".*
HERSKOVITS, MELVILLE JEAN. On the provenience of New World
Negroes [Social Forces, Chapel Hill, 12 : 247–62 : 1933–34]
*An attempt to trace areas in Africa from which American slaves
were drawn.*
JACKSON, GEORGE PULLEN. White spirituals in the Southern Uplands.
pp. 242–73. Chapel Hill : Univ. of N. Carolina Press. 1933.
*Important discussion on influence of white spirituals on Negro
religious songs.*
B., P. [i.e. PHILLIPS BARRY] Negro folk songs from Maine [Bul. Folk
Song Soc. N.E., 8 : 13–16 : 1934 ; & 9 : 10–14 : 1935]
*Brief discussion on contemporary folk songs & the origin of the
" Shout ".*
JOHNSON, GUY BENTON. Negro folk songs in the South. *In*
Culture in the South, ed. W. T. Couch. *pp.*547–69. Chapel
Hill : Univ. of N. Carolina Press. [1934]
Survey of Negro songs, their origin & development.

LAMBERT, CONSTANT. Music Ho! *pp.*201–14. Faber. 1934.
  Discusses racial characteristics in jazz.
TERRY, *Sir* RICHARD R. Voodooism in music. *pp.*1–17. Burns,
  Oates. 1934.
  Vigorously refutes theory of Negro origins of jazz.
VAN GOGH, RUPERT. The evolution of jazz [W. Afr. Review, 6 :
  15–17 : 1935]
  A popular account of Negro elements in jazz music.
HARE, MAUD CUNEY. Negro musicians & their music (African
  influences in America). 439*pp.* Washington. 1936.

2—NEGRO MUSIC IN THE WEST INDIES

(a) *Jamaica*

SLOANE, HANS. Voyage to the islands Madera, Barbados, Nieves, S.
  Christopher & Jamaica. *v.*1, *pp.*xlviii–li. For author. 1707.
  Descr. Negro songs & instr., with attempted notation of several airs.
LONG, EDWARD. The history of Jamaica. *v.*2, *pp.*423–25. Lowndes.
  1774.
  Descr. songs & instr.
BECKFORD, WILLIAM. A descriptive account of the island of Jamaica.
  *v.*1, *pp.*215–17 ; *v.*2, *p.*121. Egerton. 1790.
  *Carcmantee flute-ensemble & Whydah " bender " descr., with
  note on singing.*
RENNY, ROBERT. History of Jamaica. *pp.*168 *et seq.* Cawthorn. 1807.
  Brief account of instr. & singing.
GARDNER, WILLIAM JAMES. A history of Jamaica. *pp.*183, 386.
  Elliot Stock. 1873.
  Note on instr., copied from Long (supra).
MYERS, CHARLES SAMUEL. Traces of African melody in Jamaica.
  In JEKYLL, WALTER : Jamaican song & story [Publ. of Folk Lore
  Soc., 55] *pp.*278–85. Nutt. 1907.
  *Discussion & comparison of several melodies from Africa &
  Jamaica (latter from Sloane) : with notation.*
BECKWITH, MARTHA WARREN. Jamaica Anansi stories. 295*pp.*
  N.Y. : Amer. Folk Lore Soc. 1924.
  Gives notation of folk songs recorded on phonog. by Helen Roberts.
,, Jamaica folk-lore. 95*pp.* N.Y. : Amer. Folk Lore Soc. 1924.
  Contains music recorded in the field, by Helen Roberts.
ROBERTS, HELEN H. Some drums & drum rhythms of Jamaica [Nat.
  Hist., 24 : 241–51 : 1924] *i.*
  Several drums described, with notation of drum beats.
,, A study of folk song variants based on field work in Jamaica
  [Jour. Amer. Folklore, 38 : 149–216 : 1925]
  Includes notation of 95 airs.
,, Possible survival of African songs in Jamaica [Music. Quart.,
  12 : 340–58 : 1926]
  *Discussion of music of Maroons, with notation & analysis of
  several songs.*

BECKWITH, MARTHA WARREN & ROBERTS, HELEN H. Folk Games of Jamaica. 95*pp*. N.Y. : Amer. Folk Lore Soc. 1928.
Includes notation of many airs from phonog. recordings.
BECKWITH, MARTHA WARREN. Black roadways : a study of Jamaican folk-life. *pp*.148, 151, 192–93, 205–14. Chapel Hill : Univ. of N. Carolina Press. 1929.
Contains notation of Jamaican songs & descr. of instr.
CUNDALL, FRANK. Jamaica negro musical instr. *In* Negro anthology, ed. Nancy Cunard. *pp*.402–04. Wishart. 1934.
Suggests that instr. originating in Africa have disappeared.
ROBERTS, HELEN H. Jamaica negro " digging songs ". *In* Negro anthology, ed. Nancy Cunard. *pp*.404–05. Wishart. 1934.
Contains discussion of notation from phonog. recording.

(b) *Cuba*

ALEXANDER, JAMES EDWARD. Transatlantic sketches. *v*.1, *pp*.376–77. Bentley. 1833.
Descr. of a " Bamba ".
ORTIZ, FERNANDO. Los Negros brujos. *pp*.133–38. Madrid : Editorial América. 1905.
Instr. & dancing descr., with suggestions of Afr. survivals.
CASTELLANOS, ISRAEL. Instrumentos musicales de los afrocubanos [Archivos del Folklore Cubano, Habana, 2 : 193–208, 337–55 : 1926] *i.*
„ *Ditto : separately.* 40*pp*. Habana : Imprenta el Siglo XX. 1927. *i.*
Good descr. of instr., showing manner of construction & parallels with Afr. examples.
SÁNCHEZ de FUENTES y PELAEZ, EDUARDO. Influencia de los ritmos africanos en nuestro cancionero. 48*pp*. Habana : Imprenta el Siglo XX. 1927.
„ *Ditto. In* CARBONELL y RIVERO, J. M. : Evolución de la cultura Cubana. *v*.18, *pp*.155–202. Habana : Imprenta el Siglo XX. 1928.
Descr. dances & instr. showing Afr. characteristics, with notation of many airs.
ORTIZ, FERNANDO. El estudio de la musica afrocubana [Musicalia, Habana, 4 : 115–19 : 1928]
„ *Ditto* [La Habana, 1 : 169–74 : 1929]
Survey of ethnographical background & problems involved.
CATURLA, ALEJANDRO G. Posibilidades sinfónicas de la música afrocubana [Musicalia, Habana, 15–17 : 1929]
SANCHEZ de FUENTES y PELAEZ, EDUARDO. La canción Cubana. 46*pp*. Habana : Molina. 1930.
Discusses the influence of Afr. music on Cuban folk song, with notation.

(c) *Other Islands*

LIGON, RICHARD. A true & exact history of the island of Barbados. *pp*.48–49, 52. Humphrey Moseley. 1657.
„ Histoire de l'isle de Barbades [Recueil de divers voyages, *pp*.82–83, 1674]
Brief account of Negro drums & fifes.

Du Tertre, Jean Baptiste. Histoire générale des Antilles habitées par les François. *v.2, pp.*526–27. Paris : Jolly. 1667.
> *Brief descr. of Negro dance & music.*

Labat, Jean Baptiste. Nouveau voyage aux isles de l'Amérique. *v.4, pp.*464, 467–69 ; *v.6, p.*112. Paris : Giffart. 1742.
> *Notes on drums & guitars of Negroes of Dominica & other islands.*

Thibault de Chanvalon, *** Voyage à la Martinique. *pp.*66–67. Paris : Bauche. 1763.
> *Brief note on Negro music.*

Pinckard, George. Notes on the West Indies. *v.*1, *pp.*126–32. Baldwin. 1816.
> *Music of Barbados slaves descr.*

Bayley, F. W. N. Four years' residence in the West Indies. *pp.*436–38. Ridd. 1830.
> *Negro bands descr.*

Carmichael, *Mrs.* Domestic manners & social condition of the white, coloured & Negro population of the West Indies. *v.2, pp.*301–02. Whittaker. 1833.
> *Note on Negro song.*

Bridgens, Richard. West India scenery, with illust. of Negro character. Jennings. [? 1836]
> *See illust. of Negro dance in Trinidad, showing instr.*

Roth, Henry Ling. The aborigines of Hispaniola [R. Anthrop. Inst., 16 : 278 : 1887]
> *Descr. of Negro drum.*

Edwards, Charles L. Folklore of Bahama Negroes [Amer. Jour. Psychol., 2 : 519–28 : 1889]
> *Descr. music of clarinet, tambourines & triangle, with notation.*

Friedenthal, Albert. Stim. en der Völker : 1—Die Volksmusik der Kreolen Amerikas. 40*pp.* Berl. : Schlesinger. [1911]
> *Vol. 2 deals with Creoles of Central America, West Indies, & Venezuela, with notation of their songs.*

Panhuys, L. C. van. Muziek-instr. en muziek. *In* Encyclopaedie van Nederlandsch West-Indië, ed. H. D. Benjamins & J. F. Snelleman. *pp.*494–99. 'sGravenhage : Nijhoff. 1914–17. *bibliog.*
> *Concise descr. of Negro music & instr.*

Merwin, B. W. A voodoo drum from Hayti [Mus. Jour. Phil., 8 : 123–25 : 1917]
> *Brief descr. of drum & voodoo rites.*

Lassègue, Frank. Ciselures. 136*pp.* Albert : Grossel. 1929.
> *Includes a chapter on " La musique en Haiti ".*

Hurston, Zora Neale. Dance songs & games from the Bahamas [Jour. Amer. Folklore, 43 : 294–300 : 1930]
> *Contains notation of several dance songs.*

Bourel de la Roncière, Charles. Nègres et négriers. *pp.*121–30. Paris : Editions des Portiques. 1933. *i.*
> *Account of West African, Haiti & San Domingo instr. & music, from early travels.*

HARE, MAUD CUNEY. History & song in the Virgin Islands [Crisis, N.Y., 40 : 83–84 : 1933]
A brief popular account.

PARSONS, ELSIE CLEWS. Folklore of the Antilles, French & English, Pt.I. 521pp. N.Y. : Amer. Folk Lore Soc. 1933.
Includes notation of several songs.

ETIENNE, HENRI. Tanda : Meringue [Haiti]. *In* Negro anthology, ed. Nancy Cunard. p.406. Wishart. 1934.
Notation only.

HARE, MAUD CUNEY. Negro music in Porto Rico. *In* Negro anthology, ed. Nancy Cunard. pp.400–01. Wishart. 1934.
Notes on dances & instr.

MADIANA, *** The Biguine of the French Antilles. *In* Negro anthology, ed. Nancy Cunard. pp.401–02. Wishart. 1934.
Gives notation & comment thereon.

3—NEGRO MUSIC IN SOUTH AMERICA

(a) *Bush Negroes*

HARTSINCK, JAN JACOB. Beschryving van Guiana. v.2, pp.907–09. Amsterdam : Tielenburg. 1770.
Brief descr. of " banja ", drums & dances of Negroes.

STEDMAN, JOHN GABRIEL. Narrative of five years' expedition against the revolted negroes of Surinam in Guiana. v.2, pp.258–59, 285–87. Johnson. 1796.
Descr. singing and instr. of Saramaccaner Bush Negroes, with notations.

ALEXANDER, JAMES EDWARD. Transatlantic sketches. v.1, pp.95–96, 130. Bentley. 1833.
Incidental reference to Guiana Negro canoe song.

BENOIT, PIERRE JACQUES. Voyage à Surinam : description des possessions néerlandaises dans la Guyane. pp.23, 62 & plates 14, 40–41, 45. Brux. : Soc. des Beaux Arts. 1839.
Brief descr. of dancing & flute-playing : illust. of flutes & drums.

FOCKE, H. C. De Surinaamsche negermuzijk. *In* Bijdragen tot de bevordering van de kennis der Ned. W. Ind. kolonien. pp.93–107. Haarlem : Kruseman. 1858.
Notes on songs & instr., with four pages of notation.

COSTER, A. M. De Boschnegers in de Kolonie Suriname [Bijd. tot de taal-, land- en volkenkunde van Ned. Ind., 3 : 26–27 : 1866]
Brief descr. of Negro instr.

BONAPARTE, ROLAND NAPOLÉON. Les habitants de Suriname ; notes recueillies à l'exposition coloniale d'Amsterdam en 1883. pp.140, 171. Paris : Quantin. 1884. *i.*
Descr. Bush Negro drums, guitar, song & dancing : see illust. of drums, p.122.

CAPPELLE, HERMAN van. Bij de Indianen en Boschnegers van Suriname [Elsevier's Maandschrift, Amsterdam, 23 : 252, 310, 379 : 1902] *i.*
> *Note on drums, notation of two melodies ; illust. of drums & rattles.*

„ Au travers des forêts vierges de la Guyane hollandaise. *pp.*33, 177–78. Baarn : Impr. Hollandia. 1905.
> *Brief account of music of Bush Negro.*

PANHUYS, L. C. van. Mitteilungen über surinamsche Ethnographie und Kolonisations Geschichte : Trommelsprache [Compte Rendu, Congrès International des Américanistes, Wien, 16 : 521–26 : 1908]
> *On drums & drum language of Bush Negroes.*

„ Les chansons et la musique de la Guyane néerlandaise [Jour. Soc. Américanistes, 9 : 27–39 : 1912]
> *Includes account of Bush Negro music & songs, with notation.*

„ Boschnegers. *In* Encyclopaedie van Nederlandsch West-Indië, ed. H. D. Benjamins & J. F. Snelleman. *pp.*163, 496–98. 'sGraven-hage : Nijhoff. 1914–17.
> *Succinct account of dancing, music & song in Guiana & W. Indies.*

BOLINDER, GUSTAF. Busintana-Indianernas musikbåge. Ett bidrag till det afrikanska inflytandet på indiankulturen [Ymer, Stockholm, 37 : 300–08 : 1917] *i.*
> *Marimba & other disappearing instr. descr. : summary of article is given in French.*

LINDBLOM, GERHARD. Afrikanische Relikte und Indianische Entlehnungen in der Kultur der Busch-neger Surinams [Göteborgs K. Vetenskapsjoch vitterhets-samhället Handlingar, 28 : 58–71, 107 : 1924]
> *Descr. many instr.*

KAHN, MORTON CHARLES. Notes on the Saramaccaner Bush Negroes of Dutch Guiana [Amer. Anthrop., 31 : 485, 488 : 1929] *i.*
> *Drums & rattles descr.*

„ The Djuka. *pp.*53–62, 173–74, 189. N.Y. : Viking Press. 1931. *i.*
> *Chapter on dance & accompanying instr.; notes on flutes, drums & percussion instr.*

HERSKOVITS, MELVILLE JEAN & HERSKOVITS, FRANCES S. Rebel destiny. xvii., 366*pp.* N.Y. : McGraw Hill. 1934.
> *See index :* Dances, drums, phonograph, songs.

(b) *Latin American States*

WALSH, R. Notices of Brazil. *v.*2, *pp.*176, 335–37. Westley. 1830.
> *Brief account of guitar, sansa, monochord & drum : notation of an Afr. air.*

FINCK, GOTTLOB WILHELM. Etwas über Musik und Tanz in Brasilien [Allg. Musik. Zeit., 35 : 19–21 : 1833]
> *Descr. Negro " music bands ", an Afr. marimba, & dances of Afr. origin.*

CORTIJO, ALAHIJA. Musicologia latino-americana. *pp.*56–88, 359–80. Barcelona : Maucci. 1919.
> *General account of instr. & music.*

94

Rossi, Vicente. Cosas de negros. *pp.*339–43. Rio de la Plata :
  Imprenta Argentina. 1926.
    Account of " African " instr. in Brazil, with note on rhythms.
Nina Rodrigues, Raymundo. Os africanos no Brazil. *pp.*233–41.
  Saõ Paulo : Companhia editora nacional. 1932.
    Dancing & instr. descr. & compared with Afr. examples.
Andrade, Mario de. Essay on Brazilian music : Canto de Xangô.
  In Negro anthology, ed. Nancy Cunard. *pp.*406–07. Wishart.
  1934.
    Note on a spiritual " of Afr. origin ", with notation.

V—AFRICAN MUSIC AND THE CHURCH

Richardson, J. Malagasy " Tonon-kira " & hymnology [Antananarivo
  Annual & Madagascar Mag., 2 : 151–63 : Christmas, 1876]
    An appeal for a suitable uniform hymn-book.
Flothmeier, *** Ewe-lieder [Monatsbl. Nordd. Miss. Gesell., 71 :
  78–79 : 1910]
    Notes on the adaptation of hymn-tunes for native use, with notation.
Farrow, Stephen S. Faith, fancies & fetich : or Yoruba paganism.
  *pp.*169–75. S.P.C.K. 1924.
    Gives notation of Yoruba Christian lyrics.
Rühl, Theodor. Die missionarische Akkommodation im Gottes-
  dienstlichen Volksgesang [Zeit. f. Missionswissenschaft, 17 :
  113–35 : 1927]
    A good account of the difficulties of adaptation.
Ogumefu, Ebun. Yoruba melodies. 16*pp.* S.P.C.K. 1929.
    Contains " harmonised " notation.
Wedepohl, J. Volksmusik der Eingeborenen und Musik in Missions-
  leben und Missionskirchen auf dem Berliner Missionsfelde in
  Südafrika [Die Brücke, 6 : 4–6 : 1929]
Schlunk, Martin. Mission und Kunst [Neue Allg. Miss., 7 : 44–46 :
  1930]
    Good general discussion of the problem.
Wedepohl, J. Volksmusik der Eingeborenen in Südafrika, ihre
  Entwickelung und Verwendung in Missionsleben und Missions-
  schulen, sowie Einführung der Choralmelodien unserer Reforma-
  tions Kirche in die Missionskirche [Die Brücke, 7 : 2–3, 3–11 : 1930]
Jones, Arthur Morris. Nyimbo sya waklistu awakatoliko. 93*pp.*
  S.P.C.K. 1931.
    Lala hymn book : see preface for good statement of the possibilities
    of native hymn music. See also preface of Birkett, Christopher.
    Ingoma. Tonic Sol-fa Agency. 18 ?
Hicks, T. H. " O come let us sing " [Cent. Afr., 49 : 69–72 : 1932]
    See also letter in Cent. Afr., 51 : 56 : 1933.
Martindale, Cyril Charlie. African Angelus. *pp.*124–25, 365.
  Sheed & Ward. 1932.
    Advocates the teaching of plain-chant, adapted to native forms.

X., *pseud.* [*i.e.* A. B. Moseley] [On music] [Cent. Afr., 49 : 176–78 : 1932]
A general account.

Tracey, Hugh T. Native music & the Church [Native Teachers' Jour., 11 : 110–15 : 1932]
A plea for the encouragement of native tunes & talent.

Pulling, Grace E. The world of melody. *pp.*58–59. S.P.G. 1932.
Gives notation of W. Afr. canoe song, Central Afr. folk tunes & Kyrie eleison.

Collins, S. R. [*In* Books for Africa, 4 : 38–41 : 1934]
The writer believes that European hymns may be successfully adapted to native use.

Primitive Methodist Missionary Society. The music makers : popular report of the P.M.M.S. 156*pp.* P.M.M.S. 1934.
Contains list of (commercial) recordings of Bantu music.

Anon. [Afr. music & hymns for the Afr. church] [Books for Africa, 5 : 20–23 : 1935]
Report of a discussion on the adaptation of hymn tunes.

Duncan, J. M. [Note on European & Afr. music] [Books for Africa, 5 : 54–55 : 1935]
Brief note on native ability to learn European scale, etc.

Jones, Arthur Morris. Note on recording Afr. music & hymns [Books for Africa, 6 : 10 : 1936]

VI—DRUM LANGUAGE

Buchholz, R. Land und Leute in Westafrika [Samm. Gemein. Wiss. Vorträge Virchow & Wattenbach, ser. 11, heft 257] *pp.*46–47. Hamburg. 1876.
Note on drum signals.

Pechuel-Loesche, Edouard. Die Loango-Expedition. *v.*2, *pp.*117–19. Leip. : Frohberg. 1882.
Brief note on drum language in French Congo.

Allan, George. Notes of life in the Cameroons. *pp.*52–53. Newcastle-on-Tyne : Reid. 1885. *i.*
Duala drum & signals described.

Mähly, E. Zur Geographie und Ethnographie der Goldküste [Verh. f. Naturf. Gesell. in Basel, 7/3 : 851–52 : 1885]
Brief note on signalling.

Buchner, Max. Kamerun. *pp.*37–38. Leip. : Dunker. 1887.
On Duala signalling.

Andree, R. Signale bei Naturvölker [Zeit. f. Ethnol., 20 : 410–11 : 1888]
Notes on universality of drum language.

François, Curt von. Die Erforschung der Tschuapa und Lulongo. *p.*101. Leip. : Brockhaus. 1888.
Brief mention of Lulongo drum.

Henshaw, H. W. Drum telegraph of the Cameroon natives [Amer. Anthrop., 3 : 292 (note) : 1890]
Mention only.

MORGEN, C. Durch Kamerun von Sud nach Nord. *pp.*52–54, 197. Leip. : Brockhaus. 1893. *i.*
> *On Yaunde drum language.*

BETZ, R. Die Trommelsprache der Duala [Mitt. Schutz., 11 : 1–86 1898]
> *Good account of drums & 275 codes given, with " interpretations ".*

LANGKAVEL, BERNHARD. Afrikanische Trommeln und die Trommel-sprache [Mutter Erde, Berl., 1 : 175 : 1898] *i.*
> *Brief general account of chief types of Afr. drum.*

ZECH, *Graf* von. Vermischte Notizen über Togo und Togohinterland [Mitt. Schutz., 11 : 99, 104 : 1898]
> *Notes on drum language.*

FÜLLEBORN, FRIEDRICH. Das deutsche Njassa-Gebiet. *pp.*236, 242, 338. Berl. : Reimer. 1906. *i.*
> *Signal drums & horns descr.*

VORTISCH, H. Die Neger der Goldküste [Globus, Braunschweig, 89 : 295–96 : 1906]
> *Short notes on drum signalling.*

WESTERMANN, DIEDRICH H. Zeichensprache des Ewe-Volkes in Deutsch Togo[Mitt. Sem. Orient. Sprach. Afr. Stud., 10 : 1–14 : 1907]
> *General discussion on drum signalling.*

JOHNSTON, *Sir* HARRY HAMILTON. George Grenfell & the Congo. *v.*2, *pp.*720–21. Hutchinson. 1908.
> *Mention of signal drums.*

OVERBERGH, CYRILLE van. Les Basonge [Coll. Mon. Ethnog. 3] *pp.*344–46. Brux. 1908.
> *Summary of data concerning drum & whistle signalling.*

DELHAISE, CHARLES. Les Warega [Coll. Mon. Ethnog. 5] *p.*251. Brux. 1909.
> *Notes on drum language.*

MEYER, HANS, *ed.* Das deutsche Kolonialreich. *v.*1, *p.*490. Leip. : Bibliographisches Institut. 1909.
> *Giving distribution map (by Passarge) of drum language in Cameroons.*

OVERBERGH, CYRILLE van. Les Mangbetu [Coll. Mon. Ethnog. 4] *pp.*401–03. Brux. 1909.
> *Data on drum signalling collated.*

WARD, H. A voice from the Congo. *pp.*270–71. Heinemann. 1910.
> *Descr. a drum & its use in " drum talking ".*

WEEKS, JOHN H. Anthropological notes on the Bangala of the Upper Congo River [R. Anthrop. Inst., 40 : 404 : 1910]
> *Brief note on Bangala drum.*

WITTE, P. A. Zur Trommelsprache bei den Ewe-Leuten [Anthropos, Wien, 5 : 50–53 : 1910]
> *Several talking drums descr.*

ANON. The Call Drum [Atlantic Monthly, Boston, Mass., 107 : 140–42 : 1911]
> *Descr. social significance of drums & drum language of Bulu tribe, West Africa.*

ENGELS, *Lieut.* Les Wangata [Rev. Cong., 3 : 207–09 : 1911]
  Gives several examples of drum codes.

HALKIN, JOSEPH. Les Ababua [Coll. Mon. Ethnog. 7] *pp.* 419–20.
  Brux. 1911.
  Note on signal gongs.

HILTON-SIMPSON, MELVILLE WILLIAM. Land & peoples of the Kasai.
  *pp.*67–68, 176. Constable. 1911.
  Descr. a Batetela signal gong.

NEKES, HERMANN. Trommelsprache und Fernruf bei den Jaunde und
  Duala in Sud Kamerun [Mitt. Sem. Orient. Sprach. Afr. Stud., 15 :
  1–15, 69–83 : 1912]
  Good technical discussion, with notes on drum names.

TALBOT, PERCY AMAURY. In the shadow of the bush. *pp.*298–302.
  Heinemann. 1912.
  Gives several code messages.

MEINHOF, CARL, THILENIUS, ***, & HEINITZ, WILHELM. Die Trommelsprache in Afrika und in der Sudsee [Vox, 4 : 179–208 : 1916]

TANGHE, BASIEL. De Slang bij de Ngbandi. *pp.*58–59. Brux.,
  Goemare. 1919.
  Note on drum signalling.

HEEPE, M. Trommelsprache der Jaunde in Kamerun [Zeit. f. Eingeborenensprachen, 10 : 43–60 : 1920]
  Contains 95 code translations & comment thereon.

MIGEOD, F. W. H. Mendi drum signals [Man, 20 : 40–41 : 1920]
  Gives list of messages transmitted, but no code.

VERBEKEN, A. Le tambour-téléphone chez les indigènes de l'Afrique
  centrale [Congo, Brux., 253–84 : 1920]
  Full account of instr., system of signalling & codes.

EMPAIN, A. Les Bakela de la Loto [Soc. R. Belge Géog., 3 : 260–62 :
  1922] *i.*
  Descr. & illust. a signal gong.

LABOURET, HENRI. Langage tambouriné et sifflé [Bul. Com. Etud.,
  A.O.F., 120–58 : 1923] *bibliog. & i.*
  *Exhaustive treatment of drum & whistle language, with illust. &
  good bibliog.*

RATTRAY, ROBERT SUTHERLAND. Ashanti. Oxf. : Univ. Press. 1923.
  See index : drum language.

,, The drum language of W. Afr. [Jour. Afr. Soc., 22 : 226–36, 302–16 :
  1923] *i.*
  *Clear exposition of the use of tones, accents, etc. in drum language,
  its scope & limitations : manufacture of drums descr., with phonog.
  illust. of code messages.*

PFISTER, G. A. Les chansons historiques et le "Timpam" des
  Achantis [Rev. Music., 230–35 : 1923]
  Informative notes on Ashanti drums.

PHILIPPS, J. E. T. [Letter to Jour. Afr. Soc.] [Jour. Afr. Soc., 22 :
  343–44 : 1923]
  Notes on use of drum language in war.

CHRISTY, CUTHBERT. Big game & pygmies. *pp.*22–23, 131. Macmillan. 1924.
  Incidental remarks on Ituri drum signalling.
CZEKANOWSKI, JAN. Forschungen im Nil-Kongo-Zwischen Gebiet. *v.*6, *pt.*2, *pp.*291–93. Leip. : Klinkhardt. 1924.
  Notes on Mabudu drum language.
LINDBLOM, GERHARD. Afrikanische Relikte und Indianische Entlehnungen in der Kultur der Busch-neger Surinams [Göteborgs K. Vetenskapsjoch vitterhets-samhället Handlingar, 28/1 : 65–68 : 1924]
  A comparison of drum language in Surinam & the Gold Coast.
VERBEKEN, A. Le tambour-téléphone chez les indigènes de l'Afrique centrale [Congo, Brux., 721–28 : 1924]
  See VERBEKEN, *supra*, 1920 : *gives further examples of code messages.*
WEULE, KARL. Trommelsprache und Trommelsignale bei den Negern [Leip. Illust. Zeit., 163 : 664 : 1924]
  A general account of drum language.
BRIAULT, MAURICE. Sous le zéro équatorial. *pp.*105–12. Paris : Bloud & Gay. 1926.
  Descr. uses & occasions of drum signalling in the Congo.
TALBOT, PERCY AMAURY. Peoples of Southern Nigeria. *v.*2, *pp.*809–10. Milford. 1926.
  Gives table showing distribution of drum language.
CARDINALL, ALLAN WOLSEY. In Ashanti & beyond. *pp.*271–76. Seeley, Service. 1927.
  Notes on whistle & drum language.
G., R. de. Tribus de l'A.O.F. [Soc. Géog. Alger, 517–18 : 1927]
  Descr. several signal instr. of the Tomas.
HEINITZ, WILHELM. Ein Beitrag zum Problem der Trommelsprache [Vox, Hamburg, 9 : 29–30 : 1927]
  A footnote to work of Heepe (supra).
V., A. Die Trommelsprache der Ashanti [Zeit. f. Instrumentbau, Leip., 48 : 301–02 : 1927–28]
  Descr. work of Christaller & Rattray on drum language, with note on construction of drums.
VAN GOETHEM, L. Lokole of Tam-Tam bij de Nkundo-negers [Congo, Brux., 711–16 : 1927]
  Signal drums & code messages descr.
SPENCER PRYSE, G. Talking drums & stools of sovereignty [Illust. Lond. News, 172 : 390–91 : 1928] *i.*
BUTT-THOMPSON, FREDERICK WILLIAM. W. Afr. secret societies. *pp.*162–65. Witherby. 1929. *i.*
CHAUVET, STEPHEN. Musique nègre. *pp.*51–59. Paris : Soc. d'Editions Géog., Marit. et Col. 1929.
  Summarises data from Labouret, etc., & gives several code examples.
KAHN, MORTON CHARLES. Notes on the Saramaccaner Bush Negroes of Dutch Guiana [Amer. Anthrop., 31 : 488 : 1929]
  Brief account of drum language.

TANGHE, BASIEL. De Ngbandi naar het leven Geschetst [Congo Bibliothek] *pp.*69–70. Brugge : De Gruuthuuse Persen. 1929.
  Mention of drum signalling.

FOURNEAU, J. Des transmissions acoustiques chez les indigènes du Sud-Cameroun [Togo-Cameroun, Paris, 387–88 : 1930] *i.*
  Gives sixteen code messages.

HULSTAERT, E. P. Over de volkstammen der Lomela [Congo, Brux., 13–52 : 1931]
  Brief notes on signal instr. of Mbole, Nkonde & Bagela.

KAHN, MORTON CHARLES. The Djuka. *pp.*168–70. N.Y. : Viking Press. 1931.
  General account of drum language.

LABOURET, HENRI. Les tribus de rameau Lobi [Trav. Mém. Inst. Ethnol., *v.*15] *pp.*192–99. Paris. 1931.
  Good account of whistle language.

LABOURET, HENRI & SCHAEFFNER, ANDRÉ. Un grand tambour de bois ebrié (Côte d'Ivoire) [Bul. Mus. Ethnog. Troc., 2 : 48–55 : 1931] *bibliog. & i.*
  Descr. signal drum with a note on literature of drum language.

MEEK, CHARLES KINGSLEY. A Sudanese kingdom. *pp.*458–63. Kegan Paul. 1931.
  Gives Jukun code & many personal drum tunes.

TISSERANT, CHARLES. Essai sur la grammaire Banda [Trav. Mém. Inst. Ethnol., *v.*13] *pp.*23–24. Paris. 1931.
  Brief comments on signalling.

BAUMANN, MARGARET. Sons of sticks. *p.*34. Sheldon Press. 1933.
  Brief exposition of tone variation, as used in drum language.

BOELAERT, E. De zwarte telefoon [Congo, Brux., 356–64 : 1933]
  Drum-signalling descr.

EBOUÉ, FÉLIX. Les peuples de l'Oubangui-Chari. *pp.*80–94. Paris : Com. Afr. Franc. 1933.
  ,, *Ditto* [Rens. Col., 42 : 461–62 : 1932 ; & 43 : 14–19 : 1933]
  Note by Mme. Grall on signal instr. of Banda, with several code messages.

WIESCHHOFF, HEINZ. Die afrikanischen Trommeln und ihre ausser-afrikanischen Beziehungen. 148*pp.* Stuttgart : Strecker. 1933. *m. & i. bibliog.* 10*pp. i.*
  A detailed study of many signalling & other drums.

CLARKE, ROGER T. The drum language of the Tumba people [Amer. Jour. Sociol., 40 : 34–48 : 1934]
  Notes on manufacture of drums, manner of playing & relation between language & drum signalling.

HERZOG, GEORGE. Speech-melody & primitive music [Music. Quart. 20 : 452–66 : 1934]
  Includes good discussion of signalling & speech-tones.

TESSMAN, GÜNTER. Die Bafia. *p.*161. Stuttgart : Strecker. 1934.
  Brief mention of signal whistle.

BLEICHSTEINER, ROBERT. Das Radio des Urwalds [Atlantis, Leip., 7 : 254–56 : 1935] *i.*
A general account with good illust.

EBOUÉ, FÉLIX. La clef musicale des langages tambourinés et sifflés [Communication faite au Congrès International d'Anthrop. et d'Archéol. Préhist. de Brux., Sept. 1935]

HULSTAERT, GUSTAAF. De telefoon der Nkundo [Anthropos, Wien, 30 : 655–58 : 1935]
Detailed account of drum-codes, personal drum-tunes, etc.

LABOURET, HENRI. La langage tambouriné en Afrique [Monde Colonial Illustré, Paris, 13 : 88 : 1935]
General remarks on drum language.

LUSH, ALLAN J. Kiganda drums [Uganda Jour., 3 : 7–25 : 1935]
Manufacture & use of drums descr., with note on codes.

RATTRAY, ROBERT SUTHERLAND. What the African believes, as revealed by the talking drums [W. Afr. Rev., 6 : 12–14 : 1935]
A re-statement of conclusions regarding drum language, with a descr. of drums.

VII—COLLECTION OF MATERIAL AND PHONOGRAPH RECORDING

GARSON, JOHN GEORGE & READ, CHARLES HERCULES. Notes & queries on anthropology. *pp.*164–70. Anthrop. Inst. 1892.
Questionnaire on music compiled by C. Engel. See also 4th edition of this, ed. by Marreco & Myres. pp.214–26, 1912.

WEAD, CHARLES KASSON. The study of primitive music [Amer. Anthrop., 2 : 75–79 : 1900]
Practical advice on the recording & analysis of primitive music.

AZOULAY, ***. Sur la manière dont a été constitué le Musée Phonographique de la Société d'Anthropologie [Bul. Soc. Anthrop. Paris, 5 : 305–20, 327–29 : 1901]

,, Liste de phonogrammes composant le Musée Phonographique de la Société d'Anthropologie [Bul. Soc. Anthrop. Paris, 5 : 652–65 : 1902]
Includes about fifty African records.

ABRAHAM, O. & HORNBOSTEL, ERICH M. von. Über die Bedeutung des Phonographen für vergleichende Musikwissenschaft [Zeit. f. Ethnol., 36 : 222–36 : 1904]
Explains use of phonog. & theory of tone systems, giving specimen investigation sheet.

LUSCHAN, FELIX von. Anleitung für ethnographische Beobachtung und Sammlungen in Afrika und Oceanien. *pp.*58–65. Berl. : K. Mus. f. Völkerkunde. 1904.
Questionnaire & suggestive notes for the field-worker in primitive music.

ABRAHAM, O. & HORNBOSTEL, ERICH M. von. Über die Harmonis-erierbarkeit exotischer Melodien [Sammelbände der Internationalen Musikgesellschaft, Leip., 7 : 138–41 : 1905]
Detailed technical notes on transcription.

READ, CHARLES HERCULES. Anthropological queries for Central Africa. *p.*17. British Museum. 1905.
Includes questionnaire on music & instr.

GODDARD, PLINY EARLE. A graphic method of recording songs. *In* Anthropological papers written in honour of F. Boas. *pp.*137–42. N.Y. : Stechert. 1906.
Exposition of kymograph recording.

MYERS, CHARLES SAMUEL. The ethnological study of music. *In* Anthropological papers presented to E. B. Tylor. *pp.*235–53. Oxf. : Clarendon Press, 1907.
On the importance of studying primitive music : with appendix on use of phonog., and methods of transcription.

STUMPF, CARL. Das Berliner Phonogramm-Archiv [Internationale Wochenschrift, 2 : 226–40 : 1908]
A historical & descriptive account, with notes on the use of the phonog.

WALLASCHEK, RICHARD. Über den Wert phonographischer Aufnahmen von Gesängen der Naturvölker [Compte Rendu, Congrès International des Américanistes, Wien, 16 ; 557–61 : 1908]
Short discussion on uses & abuses of phonog.

ABRAHAM, O. & HORNBOSTEL, ERICH M. von. Vorschläge für die Transkription exotischer Melodien [Sammelbände der Internationalen Musikgesellschaft, Leip. 11 : 1–25 : 1909]
Gives rules for transcription of phonog. records, with detailed notes on tone, phrasing, rhythm, tempo, etc.

AZOULAY, *** Les musées et archives phonographiques avant et depuis la fondation du Musée Phonographique de la Société d'Anthropologie, 1900 [Bul. Soc. Anthrop. Paris, 6 : 450–57 : 1911]
Descr. the formation of phonog. archives in the United States, Hungary, and at Vienna.

FOUCART, GEORGE. Introductory questions on African ethnology. *pp.*134–36. Cairo : Soc. Sult. Géog. 1919.
Brief questionnaire on native music, instr. & singing.

HEINITZ, WILHELM. Phonogramme. *In* Im Hochland von Mittel, kamerun, pt.3. *pp.*143–45, *et seq.* [Abh. Hamburger Kol. Inst. 41] 1919.
Notes on the use & limitations of the phonograph.

THALBITZER, WILLIAM. The phonograph & the human ear as rival means of recording music & language [Kommissionen for ·Ledelsen af de geologiske . . . Undersøgelser i Grønland, *v.*40] *pp.*544–59. København. 1923.
A technical discussion with practical examples.

CLOSSON, ERNEST. Questionnaire d'ethnographie : musique [Soc. R. Belge Géog., 49 : 132–43 : 1925]
Deals with music, singing & instr.

PASCHE, *** Phonographische Systeme und Probleme [Signale f. die musikalische Welt, 85 : 737–39 : 1926–27]
Discusses technical problems of the phonog.

HAJEK, LEO. Das Phonogrammarchiv der Akad. der Wiss. in Wien von seiner Gründung bis zur Neueinrichtung i. J. 1927 [Akad. Wiss. in Wien, phil. hist. Klasse, Sitz. 207] 22*pp*. Wien. 1927.
Good historical & descriptive account of the Vienna & other archives.

METFESSEL, MILTON. The collecting of folk songs by phonophotography [Science, Lancaster, Pa., 67 : 28–31 : 1928]
,, Phonophotography in folk music : American negro songs in new notation. 192*pp*. Chapel Hill : Univ. of N. Carolina Press. 1928. *i.*
Technique & advantages of direct photography of the voice described.

SEASHORE, CARL E. Three new approaches to the study of negro music [Ann. Amer. Acad. Polit. Soc. Sci., 140 : 191–92 : 1928]
Discusses phonophotography & other " measures of musical talent ".

COEUROY, ANDRÉ & CLARENCE, G. Le phonographe. 194*pp*. Paris : Kra. 1929.
Chapter 5 deals with phonog. archives.

HERZOG, GEORGE. [*Review of* METFESSEL, M. : Phonophotography in folk music] [Jour. Amer. Folklore, 43 : 219–23 : 1930]
Defines limitations of phonog. recording.

PARIS—*Musée d'Ethnographie du Trocadéro.* Instructions sommaires pour les collecteurs d'objets ethnographiques. *pp*.18–19. Paris. 1931.
Questionnaire on dancing & instr.

ROBERTS, HELEN H. Suggestions to field-workers in collecting folk-music & data about instr. [Poly. Soc., 40 : 103–28 : 1931]
Useful notes on approach to natives, details of recording & equipment : hints on notation, transcription, etc.

HAJEK, LEO. Das Phonogramm-Archiv der Akad. der Wiss. in Wien [Zeit. f. Vergleich. Musikwiss., 1 : 15–16 : 1933]
Brief account of equipment, resources & staff.

HORNBOSTEL, ERICH M. von. Das Berliner Phonogrammarchiv [Zeit. f. Vergleich. Musikwiss., 1 : 40–45 : 1933]
Historical account of archives, list of field workers attached, & publications based on the archives, with a classified list of resources.

HERZOG, GEORGE. Recording primitive music in Africa & America [Bul. Folk Song Soc. N.E., 8 : 2–3 : 1934]
Good discussion on methods of approach & supernatural nature of songs.

KORNERUP, THORWALD. Acoustic methods of work in relation to systematic comparative musicology. 56*pp*. København : Jørgensen. 1934.
A technical discussion on acoustics in recording.

HERZOG, GEORGE. Research in primitive & folk-music in the U.S. [Amer. Council of Learned Societies, Wash., Bull. 24] 97*pp*. Wash. 1936.
A stimulating survey of work achieved & outstanding, with good lists of phonog. records & select bibliographies.

Jones, Arthur Morris. Note on recording Afr. music [Books for Africa, 6 : 10 : 1936]

Vox. Mitteilungen aus dem Phonetischen Laboratorium, Hamburg, 1920- [*In continuation*] Hamburg, 1920-

VIII—CLASSIFICATION AND ARRANGEMENT OF MATERIAL

Chouquet, Gustave. Le Musée du Conservatoire National de Musique : catalogue descriptif et raisonné. *pp.*197–256. Paris : Firmin-Didot. 1884. *i.*
> *An interesting attempt to classify "instr. of non-European countries".*

Hornbostel, Erich M. von & Sachs, Curt. Systematik der Musikinstrumente [Zeit. f. Ethnol., 46 : 553–90 : 1914]
> *Criticises earlier schemes of classification & constructs another, according to the characteristics Idio-, Membrano-, Chordo-, & Aero-phone : localities shown.*

Sachs, Curt. Die Hornbostel-Sachs'sche Klassifikation der Musikinstrumente [Naturwissenschaften, Berl., 51 : 1056–59 : 1914]
> *Gives short history of previous schemes & exposition of new classification.*

Montandon, George. La genéalogie des instruments de musique et les cycles de civilisation [Archiv. Suisses Anthrop. Générale, 3/1 : 1–120 : 1919]
> *Classification is intended to show evolution of musical instr. according to culture cycles : with special reference to sansas. For critiques of Montandon, see : Schmidt, P. G. in Anthropos, v.14–15, pp.565–70, 1919–20 ; and Vernau, R. in L'Anthrop., v.30, pp.192–95, 1919.*

Schaeffner, André. Des instruments de musique dans un musée d'ethnographie [Documents, Paris, 5 : 248–54 : 1929] *i.*
> *Discussion on difficulties of arrangement, & value of ethnographical study of music.*

Sachs, Curt. Geist und Werden der Musikinstrumente. 282*pp.* Berl. : Reimer. 1929. *bibliog.* 17*pp.*
> *Traces the evolution of musical instr. in relation to civilisation : carefully notes & tabulates their distribution : for critique of Sachs, see Montandon, G. in L'Anthrop., v.39, pp.557–59, 1929, & Lachmann, R., in Zeit. f. Musikwiss, v.12, pp.494–97, 1929.*

Schaeffner, André. Projet d'une classification nouvelle des instr. de musique [Bul. Mus. Ethnog. Troc., 1 : 21–25 : 1931]
> *Outline of classification scheme given infra.*

Norlind, Tobias. Musikinstrumentensystematik [Svensk Tidskrift f. Musikforskning, Stockholm, 1–4, 95–123 : 1932]
> *Classification by auto-, areo- & chordo-phone.*

Schaeffner, André. D'une nouvelle classification méthodique des instruments de musique [Rev. Music., 13 : 215–31 : 1932]
> *Suggests classification according to methods of vibration.*

HORNBOSTEL, ERICH M. von. The ethnology of African sound instr. [Africa, 5 : 129–54, 277–311 : 1933]

> *Important attempt to group African instr. in relation to their extra-African distribution : with glossary.*

SCHAEFFNER, ANDRÉ. Note sur la filiation des instruments à cordes. *In* Mélanges du musicologie offerts à M. Lionel de la Laurencie. *pp.*287–94. Paris : Publications de la Soc. Franc. de Musicologie. 1933.

> *Suggests that string-attachment should be the criterion for classification, not the material used.*

IX—LIST OF MUSEUMS CONTAINING INSTRUMENTS

ABERDEEN—*Marischal College Anthropological Museum.* Illustrated catalogue. *pp.*299, 305, 317, 327, 336. Aberdeen. 1912. *i.*

BASEL—*Evangelische Missions Gesellschaft.* Katalog der ethnographischen Sammlung im Museum des Missionhauses zu Basel. *p.*25. Basel. 1883.

BERLIN—*Museum für Völkerkunde.* Vorläufiger Führer durch das Mus. für Völk. *pp.*116–145. Berl. 1925.

BERLIN—*Staatliche Hochschule für Musik.* Sammlung alter Musikinstr. bei den Staatlichen Hochschule für Musik : Beschreibender Katalog ; by Curt Sachs. *pp.*317–46. Berl. : Bard. 1922. *i.*

BERN—*Historisches Museum.* Die ethnographische Abteilung ; by R. Zeller. *In* Jahrb. d. Bernischen Hist. Museum in Bern, 1929. *pp.*154–63. 1930.

> *Mentions several African instr.*

BRUXELLES—*Musée Instrumentale du Conservatoire Royale du Musée de Bruxelles.* Catalogue descriptif et analytique du Musée Instrumentale ; by V. C. Mahillon. 4v. Ghent. 1909.

> *Many references to African instr.*

CHICAGO—*Field Museum of Natural History.* African musical instr. [Field Museum News, 5/8 : 3 : 1934]

COPENHAGEN. *See* KØBENHAVN.

DRESDEN—*Museen für Tierkunde & Völkerkunde.* [Contains a number of Afr. instr.]

EDINBURGH—*Royal Scottish Museum.* Guide to the gallery of comparative ethnography. *pp.*20–23. Edinburgh : H.M.S.O. 1928.

FIRENZE—*Collezione Etnografico-Musicale Kraus.* Catalogo. *pp.*12–13. Firenze : Landi. 1901.

FIRENZE—*Museo Nazionale d'Antropologia.* Gli oggetti musicali del Mus. Nazionale d'Antrop ; by N. Puccioni. [Archiv. Antrop. Etnol., 36 : 70–75, 80 : 1906] *bibliog.*

FRANKFURT-am-MAIN—*Forschungsinstitut für Kulturmorphologie.* [Contains drums, stringed instr., sansas & marimbas]

FRANKFURT-am-MAIN—*Städtisches Völkermuseum.* Beiträge zur Musik-instrumenten-Forschung ; by J. Lehmann (supra). *pp.*113–25. Frankfurt-a.-M. 1925.

GENÈVE—*Musée Ethnographique de Genève.* Catalogue raisonné des instr. de musique ; by G. Montandon. [Archiv. Suisses d'Anthrop. Générale, 3 : 95–118 : 1919]

HAMBURG—*Museum für Völkerkunde.* Strukturprobleme in primitiver musik ; by W. Heinitz. *pp.*197–98. Hamburg : Friederichsen. 1931.

HAMPTON, Virginia—*Hampton Institute.* Some musical instr. of the primitive African ; by Sara Lane [S. Workman, 56 : 552–56 : 1927] *i.*

KØBENHAVŃ—*Carl Claudius' Samling af Gamle Musikinstrumente.* [Catalogue] *pp.*382–89. København. 1931.

KØBENHAVN—*Musikhistorisk Museum.* Das Musikhistorische Museum, Kopenhagen ; by A. Hammerich. *pp.*130 *et seq.* Leip. : Breitkopf. 1911.

KÖLN—*Museum für Völkerkunde.* Führer durch das Rautenstrauch-Joest-Museum der Stadt Cöln ; by W. Foy. *pp.*171–210. Köln. 1908. *i.*

LEIDEN—*Rijks Ethnographisch Museum.* Ethnographisch Album van het Stroomgebied van den Congo ; by J. D. E. Schmeltz. Plates 183–98. 'sGravenhage. 1904–16.

LEIPZIG—*Museum für Völkerkunde.*

LIVERPOOL—*Public Museums.* Handbook & guide to African collection ; by J. Withers Gill. *pp.*16–17. Liverpool. 1931.

LONDON—*British Museum.* Handbook to the ethnographical collections. 319*pp.* 1925. *i.*

LONDON—*Horniman Museum.* Guide to the collections in the Horniman Museum. *pp.*25–34. 4th ed. London County Council. 1936.

LONDON—*South Kensington Museum.* A descriptive catalogue of the musical instr. in the South Kensington Museum. *pp.*141–56. Eyre & Spottiswoode. 1874. *i.*

MICHIGAN—*Stearns Collection.* Catalogue of the Stearns Collection of musical instr. ; by A. A. Stanley. Ann Arbor : Univ. of Michigan. 1918. *bibliog.* 11*pp.*
  See index under Africa.

OXFORD—*Pitt Rivers Museum.* [Contains a number of Afr. instr. *See also* BALFOUR (*supra*)]

MILANO—*Museo del Conservatorio di Milano.* Gli strumenti musicali nel Museo del Conservatorio di Milano ; by U. Hoepli. *pp.*56, 62, 63, 66, 70. Milano. 1908]

NEW YORK—*Metropolitan Museum of Art.* Catalogue of ́ Crosby Brown Collection of musical instr. of all nations : III—Instr. of savage tribes & semi-civilised peoples, pt.1—Africa. 79*pp.* N.Y. 1907. *i.*

PARIS—*Musée du Conservatoire Nationale de Musique.* Catalogue descriptif ; by G. Chouquet. *pp.*197–256. Paris. 1884.

PARIS—*Musée d'Ethnographie du Trocadéro.* [Contains Afr. instr. *See also* SCHAEFFNER (*supra*)]

PARIS—*De Léry Collection.* Catalogue des anciens instruments de musique. *pp.* 10-11, 140–41, 144–47, 156. Paris. 1910.

Sundsvall—*Etnografiska Samlingar.* Afrikanska musikinstrument i Sundsvalls läroverks etnografiska Samlingar ; by D. Frylkund. 22*pp*. Sundsvall. 1915.

Washington—*U.S. National Museum.* Handbook of collection of musical instr. in U.S. National Museum ; by F. Densmore [U.S. Nat. Mus. Bul. 136] 164*pp*. Wash. 1927. *i.*

Wien—*Kunsthistoriches Museum.* Die Sammlung alter Musikinstr. ; by J. Schlosser. 143*pp*. Wien. 1920.

See references to African instr.

X—BIBLIOGRAPHIES

Asiatica. A monthly record of literature dealing with the East and with Africa, 1928—[*In continuation*] London. 1928—

Bibliographie éthnographique du Congo belge et des régions avoisinantes, 1925–30 [Mus. Congo Belge] xi.358*pp*. Brux. [1932]

„ for 1931. 88*pp*. Brux. 1933.

„ for 1932. 112*pp*. Brux. 1933.

The bibliography is in continuation.

Endo, Hirosi. Bibliography of oriental & primitive music. 62*pp*. Tokio : Azabu-Ku. 1929.

Ethnologisches Anzeiger, 1926—[*In continuation*] Stuttgart. 1926.—

Herzog, George. Research in primitive & folk music in the U.S. [Amer. Council of Learned Societies, Wash., Bull. 24] *pp*.85–93. 1936.

Excellent select list of Negro folk songs & recordings.

Knosp, Gaston. Bibliographia exotica [Supplt. to S.I.M., Paris, *v*.6, *p*.18, Nov. 1910]

Lester, P. Bibliographie africaniste [Jour. Soc. Africanistes, 1 : 315–428 : 1931, *et seq*]

Mattfeld, Julius. The folk music of the Western hemisphere : a list of references in the N.Y. Public Library. *pp*.10–11, 38–46. N.Y. 1935.

Sachs, Curt. Geist und Werden der Musikinstrumente. 282*pp*. Berl. : Reimer. 1929. *bibliog.* 17*pp*.

A detailed bibliog. of Afr. instr.

Schapera, Isaac. Select bibliography : the present state & future development of ethnographical research in S. Afr. [Bantu Stud., 8 : 280–342 : 1934]

White, Newman Ivey. American Negro folk-songs. *pp*.469–80. Camb. : Harvard U. P. 1928.

Work, Monroe Nathan. A bibliography of the Negro in Africa & America. xxii.698*pp*. N.Y. : Wilson. 1928.

Zeitschrift für Vergleichende Musikwissenschaft. *Published by* Gesellschaft zur Erforschung der Musik des Orients, 1933—[*In continuation*] Berl. 1933—

Contains the most comprehensive available bibliography, well compiled.

Zeitschrift für Musikwissenschaft. *Published by* Deutsche Musikgesellschaft, 1918—[*In continuation*] Leip. 1918—

See cumulative bibliographies.

XI.—AUTHOR INDEX.

Abadie, M. 35.
Abraham, O. 101(2), 102.
Abraham, R. C. 46.
Adam, P. 37.
Adams, W. 19, 24.
Aitchison, S. G. G. 82.
Alakija, O. A. 23.
Albéca, A. L. de. 40.
Alberti, L. 79.
Alexander, *Sir* J. E. 71(2), 91, 93.
Allan, G. 96.
Allen, W. 47.
Ambros, A. W. 19.
Amu, E. 23, 43.
Anderson, A. A. 84.
Andersson, C. J. 72.
Andrade, M. de. 95.
Andree, R. 96.
Angas, G. F. 81.
Angelo, M. 51.
Ankermann, B. 24, 25(3), 48.
Antheil, G. 58.
Arbousset, J. T. 79, 83.
Arnoux, A. 59.
Ashe, T. 86.
Avelot, R. 49.
Azoulay, ***. 101(2), 102.
Azŭ, E. 43.

Backhouse, J. 79.
Baeyens, M. 56.
Baglioni, S. 25.
Bailly, E. 37.
Baines, T. 72.
Baker, *Sir* S. W. 29(2).
Balfour, H. 24, 25, 75, 80.
Ballanta, N. G. J. 33(3), 87.
Barbot, J. 42.
Bardi, B. 28.
Barnard, *Lady* A. 80.
Barret, P. 49.
Barrett, J. O. W. 68.
Barrington, G. 78.
Barrow, *Sir* J. 78.
Barry, P. 89.
Barton, W. E. 87.

Basden, G. T. 45.
Bastian, A. 70.
Bastos, A. 70.
Bastos, M. H. C. 69(3).
Baumann, H. 31, 71(2).
Baumann, M. 46, 100.
Baumann, O. 51(2), 63(2).
Bayley, F. W. N. 92.
Bazin, H. 34.
Beckford, W. 90.
Beckwith, M. W. 90(2), 91(2).
Beecham, J. 42.
Béguin, E. 74.
Bellile, ***. 37.
Benoît, P. J. 93.
Bent, J. T. 28, 74.
Bentley, W. H. 51.
Bérenger-Feraud, L. J. D. 37(2).
Bernard, ***. 54.
Bernatzik, H. A. 31, 36(3), 58.
Bertrand, A. 74.
Betz, R. 97.
Beutler, V. A. F. 78.
Bieber, F. J. 28.
Binger, L. G. 34.
Bingham, W. V. 20.
Bissuel, H. 34.
Bittremieux, L. 55.
Bleek, D. F. 71(2), 80(2), 81.
Bleek, E. 80.
Bleek, W. H. I. 80.
Bleichsteiner, R. 101.
Boelaert, E. 100.
Boilat, P. D. 37.
Bolinder, G. 94.
Bonaparte, R. N. 93.
Bonanni, F. 24.
Borcherds, P. B. 79.
Bosman, W. 42.
Bouche, P. 40.
Boulton, L. C. 46.
Bourel de la Roncière, C. 92.
Bowdich, T. E. 42(2).
Briault, M. 99.
Bridgenš, R. 92.
Brisley, T. 38.
Brown, M. E. 19, 24.

109

Goldstein, W. 87.
Gorer, G. 33.
Gouldsbury, C. 74.
Grandidier, A. & G. 85.
Granner, E. 37.
Grant, J. A. 59, 63.
Gray, W. G. 36.
Grébert, F. 50(2).
Gretschel, E. 80.
Griaule, M. 29.
Gröben, O. F. von der. 41.
Grosse, E. 19.
Grout, L. 81.
Güssfeldt, P. 49.
Guiral, L. 49.

Hagemann, C. 65.
Hahn, T. 72(2), 79.
Hajdukiewicz, de Pomian, A. 40.
Hajek, L. 103(2).
Halkin, J. 55(2), 98.
Hall, H. U. 46, 57.
Hambly, W. D. 21, 46, 71(2).
Hammar, J. 53.
Hammerich, A. 106.
Hare, M. C. 21, 25(2), 87, 90, 93(2).
Harfeld, le Commandant. 56.
Harris, P. G. 46.
Harrison, J. J. 53.
Harroy, F. 53.
Hartmann, R. 24, 29.
Hartsinck, J. J. 93.
Hecquard, H. 37.
Heepe, M. 98.
Heilborn, A. 39, 72.
Heim, A. 39.
Heinitz, W. 22, 26, 27, 29, 32, 35, 40, 48, 66, 98, 99, 102, 106.
Hellwald, F. von. 80.
Henrici, E. 39.
Henry, J. 34.
Henshaw, H. W. 96.
Herold, ***. 39.
Herrmann, ***. 63.
Herscher-Clément, ***. 29.
Herskovits, M. J. 89(2), 94.
Herskovits, F. S. 94.

Herzog, G. 67(2), 100, 103(3), 107.
Hichens, W. 22.
Hicks, T. H. 95.
Hilton-Simpson, M. W. 55, 98.
Hinde, H. & S. L. 62.
Hobley, C. W. 60, 62(2).
Hoepli, U. 106.
Hösemann, ***. 47.
Hofmayr, W. 30.
Holden, W. C. 82.
Holland, T. 67.
Hollis, Sir A. C. 62.
Holub, E. 73(2), 74.
Hornbostel, E. M. von. 20(2), 21, 26, 40, 50, 59, 64(2), 86, 88(2), 101(2), 102, 103, 104,105.
Hossfeld, C. 64.
Hovelacque, A. 33.
Hübbe-Schleiden, K. 49.
Hulstaert, E. P. 100.
Hulstaert, G. 58, 101.
Humbert-Savageot, M. 41.
Huot, L. 21.
Hurston, Z. N. 92.
Hutter, F. 47(2).

Idelsohn, A. Z. 69.
Immenroth, W. 58.
Ingrams, W. H. 67(2).
Iradier, M. 51.
Irle, I. 72.
Isert, P. E. 33.
Ivens, R. 70.

Jackson, G. P. 89(2).
Jacques, V. 63.
Jaeger, F. 65.
Jalla, L. 75.
Jaspert, F. & W. 71.
Jean, C. C. 34.
Jeanneret, P. 68.
Jekyll, W. 90.
Jobson, R. 36.
Johnson, G. B. 88(4), 89(3).
Johnson, J. W. 88.
Johnson, S. 45.
Johnson, T. B. 60.

111

112

Valdez, S. T.   70.
Valentyn, F.   77.
Van den Bergh, L. J.   62.
Van den Plas, J.   30.
Van der Burgt, J. M. M.   58, 59.
Van Goethem, L.   99.
Van Gogh, R.   90.
Van Hoepen, A. E.   85.
Van Mol, O. P.   57, 58.
Van Warmelo, N. J.   85.
Vedder, H.   73.
Védy, ***.   53(2).
Verbeken, A.   57, 98, 99.
Vereyecken, ***.   52.
Verneau, R.   28, 104.
Verneuil, V.   36.
Viaene, E.   54.
Villault, *le Sieur*.   32.
Villoteau, G. A.   29.
Vischer, H.   44.
Von Rosen, E.   74.
Vortisch, H.   43, 97.

Wallaschek, R.   19, 24, 102.
Walsh, R.   94.
Wangemann, H. T.   84.
Ward, H.   54, 97.
Ward, W. E. F.   43, 44(2), 89.
Waterhouse, G.   77.
Watson, J. T.   23.
Wead, C. K.   101.
Webb, M.   76.
Weber, W.   21(2), 22, 66.
Webster, W. H. B.   79.
Wedepohl, J.   95(2).
Weeks, J. H.   54, 55, 56, 97.

Weiss, M.   60, 64.
Wendt, T.   76.
Werner, A.   38, 62, 66, 67, 83.
Werner, H.   72.
Werth, E.   65, 67.
Werther, C. W.   63.
Wessmann, R.   84.
Westermann, D. H.   35, 97.
Weule, K.   39, 64(2), 66, 99.
Wheeler, A. J.   25.
White, N. I.   87, 88, 107.
Widdicombe, J.   84.
Widenmann, A.   63.
Wieschhoff, H.   26, 100.
Williams, L. H.   33.
Wilson, C. T.   59.
Wilverth, ***.   52.
Winkelman, F. von.   78.
Winterbottom, T. M.   41.
Wintersgill, H. G.   53.
Wissmann, H.   52.
Witte, P. A.   40, 97.
Wolf, L.   52.
Wood, J. G.   19.
Work, M. N.   20, 107.
Worthington, E. B. & S.   62.

Young, T. C.   67.

Zech, *Graf* von.   97.
Zeller, R.   43, 105.
Zenker, G.   47.
Zerwick, ***.   83.
Zöllner, H.   29.
Zucchelli, A.   69.
Zuure, B.   59(2).